YESTERDAY'S VOICES ON THE INNER LIFE
Volume Two
A Prose and Poetry Anthology

YESTERDAY'S VOICES ON THE INNER LIFE

Volume Two

A Prose and Poetry Anthology

Compiled by A. A. Willis

Yesterday's Voices on the Inner Life: Volume Two
Copyright © 2021 by A. A. Willis

All rights reserved. This book or any portion thereof may not be reproduced or used in any manner whatsoever without the express written permission of the publisher, except for the use of brief quotations in a book review.

Printed in the United States of America

Luminare Press
442 Charnelton St.
Eugene, OR 97401
www.luminarepress.com

LCCN: 2019910575
ISBN: 978-1-64388-881-1

......*whatsoever things are true, whatsoever things are honest, whatsoever things are just, whatsoever things are pure, whatsoever things are lovely, whatsoever things are of good report; if there be any virtue, and if there be any praise, think on these things.*

—Philippians 4:8. KJV.

Table of Contents

Introduction 1

Part One
On Mind, Thought, the Inner Life

1. On Mind, Thought, Introspection 7
2. On the Inner Journey, the Spiritual Path, the Spiritual Quest 16
3. On Philosophy 21
4. On Wisdom 25
5. On Prayer, Meditation, Reflection 32
6. On Conscience, the Inner Voice 40

Part Two
On the Nature of Things

7. On the Lessons of Nature 49
8. On the Mysteries of Life 63
9. On Higher Laws, Unseen Order, Divine Order 71
10. On Change, Rhythms, Ebb and Flow, Cycles 80

11. On Impermanence, Mortality,
    the March of Time 86

12. On Unity, Oneness 91

13. On Cause and Effect, Conditionality,
    Interdependence 100

14. On Reading, Books, Literature 104

15. On Poetry and Poets 112

16. On Work, Labor, Toil 124

17. On Time 131

18. On Music, Song, Dance 139

Part Three
On Character, Conduct, Virtues

19. On the Golden Mean, Moderation,
    Temperance, the Middle Way 151

20. On Gratitude, Thankfulness 156

21. On Courage, Strength of Spirit 162

22. On Non-Attachment, Detachment,
    Letting Go 170

23. On Happiness, Contentment 174

24. On Sorrows and Joys 180

25. On Giving, Charity, Generosity 186

26. On Duty, Service 191

27. On Virtue and Virtues 198

28. On Talking, Speech, Words 205

29. On Silence 210

30. On Serenity, Inner Peace, Equanimity,
    Tranquility 214

31. On Simplicity, Small Things, the Essentials ... 219

32. On Patience, Waiting, Forbearance 226

33. On Humility, Humbleness 232

34. On Kindness, Benevolence,
    Compassion, Mercy 238

35. On Successful Living, Living
    With Purpose 245

References 251

INTRODUCTION

THROUGHOUT HISTORY ENLIGHTENED MEN AND WOMEN have given us a vast treasury of inspirational and thought-provoking literature designed to help us navigate through, and alleviate the burdens of, our journey through life. As a companion to the first *Yesterday's Voices on the Inner Life* prose and poetry anthology, this second volume continues with more selections illustrating the timeless themes on the inner life to be found in the world's literature of the past. These verse and prose selections focus on the world of mind and thought, on our connections with the external world, and on our human condition and conduct. The hope is that the items in this second collection can also offer inspiration, guidance, and comfort for the reader in our rapidly changing times.

Down through the centuries, prose and poetry that speaks to our inner being has been an invaluable guide for seeking peace of mind, pursuing a successful life, and living with purpose and meaning. Men and women sages, thinkers, philosophers, clerics, and poets have left a vast and rich tapestry of this literature for those who have chosen to give attention to essential aspects of the inner life.

Continuing the format of the first compilation, this second volume has three primary sections: "Mind, Thought, the Inner Life", "the Nature of Things", and "Character, Conduct, Virtues". These categories are complementary and inter-connected. This collection displays the parallels, syncretism, and harmonies that can be found among the various spiritual, philosophical, poetic, and religious traditions that have originated throughout our history. These harmonies and connections are illustrated by poets and thinkers of all eras as they have addressed the enduring principles of unity and oneness in our world. Contained in this second volume are more selections from spiritual traditions, philosophical schools, and from writers such as Emerson, Shakespeare, and other well-known and lesser-known names from history that have contributed to this legacy.

The enlightened minds of ancient and more modern times offer perspectives and insights by their timeless words that continue to supply guidance for navigating through life's journey in our present day. Their many viewpoints, in verse and prose, on universal themes and truths can prove worthwhile for reflection, and for practice to those on the path to inner peace, greater wisdom, and deeper awareness.

On reading literature anthologies targeted to our inner life, it has been well-written by James Mudge in the preface to his poetry anthology published in 1909:

"It should be said, though it is perhaps hardly necessary, that this is by no means a book to be read at a sitting……….. It can be taken with largest profit only a little at a time, according as the mood demands and circumstances appoint. There should be very much meditation mingled with the perusal, an attempt to penetrate the deep meaning of the lines and have them enter into the soul for practical benefit." (James Mudge. "Preface." *Poems with Power to Strengthen the Soul.*)

How the power of words can uplift our spirit and inspire us has given us offerings from the world's awakened and liberated souls down through the centuries for our benefit in these present times. The same themes recur again and again in literature on the beneficial aspects of giving regular attention to the inner life of the individual and its connection to the collective well-being. Studying, and being receptive to, the wisdom and lessons of history's enduring literature can be a valuable guiding light on our journey, "sacred communications across the ages."

—A. A. Willis
2021

Part One

ON MIND, THOUGHT, THE INNER LIFE

Chapter 1

On Mind, Thought, Introspection

The fine associations of the Mind,
With their own loveliness, invest each hue
And form of nature!—Unless thus combined
With feelings holy,—eloquent,—and true,
What were this gorgeous firmament of blue—
These floating mountains of a vapoury sphere—
This commonwealth of flowers,—this vast review
Of worldly splendor, bursting far and near?
Oh! what were Earth itself, unless the Mind were here?

—Charles Swain.
"The Mind." *The Mind, and Other Poems.*

Life is not all incident; it has its intervals of thought, as well as action—of feeling—of endurance; and in order to reflect, and profit by these, it is sometimes necessary to sit down as it were upon the sand-hills of the desert, and consider from what point in the horizon the journey has been made, or to what opening in the distance it is likely to lead.

—Sarah Stickney Ellis (Mrs. Ellis).
"Chapter XXXV." *Hearts and Homes; or Social Distinction. A Story.*

You cannot master yourself unless you know yourself. There are mirrors for the face but none for the mind. Let careful thought about yourself serve as a substitute. When the outer image is forgotten, keep the inner one to improve and perfect.

—Baltasar Gracián.
The Art of Worldly Wisdom.

The mind is a little universe. Cheerfulness may be likened to an auspicious star or cloud; anger to thunder or a torrential rain; benevolence to a genial wind or a sweet dew; rigor to the burning sun or the killing frost of autumn. Cheerfulness, anger, mercy, severity—who can be without these emotions? Only what is necessary is to see that any of these passions should not stay too long in the mind but that they should follow one another in due proportion, so as to keep the heart always open and unobstructed. It is only in such a happy state that the mind can be at one with the cosmos.

—Hung Ying-Ming.
Musings of a Chinese Vegetarian.

From Nature doth emotion come, and moods
Of calmness equally are Nature's gift:
This is her glory; these two attributes
Are sister horns that constitute her strength.
Hence Genius, born to thrive by interchange
Of peace and excitation, finds in her
His best and purest friend; from her receives
That energy by which he seeks the truth,

From her that happy stillness of the mind
Which fits him to receive it when unsought.

—WILLIAM WORDSWORTH.
"Book Thirteenth." *The Prelude, or Growth of a Poet's Mind.*

With mind, delineate mind; and dare define
The point, where human mingles with divine:
Majestic still, her solemn form shall stand,
To shew the beacon on the distant land—
Of thought, and nature, chronicler sublime!
The world her lesson, and her teacher Time!

—ELIZABETH BARRETT BROWNING.
"An Essay on Mind." *An Essay on Mind, with Other Poems.*

Tempest-tossed souls, wherever ye may be, under whatsoever conditions ye may live, know this - in the ocean of life the isles of Blessedness are smiling, and sunny shore of your ideal awaits your coming. Keep your hand firmly upon the helm of thought. In the bark of your soul reclines the commanding Master; He does but sleep; wake Him. Self-control is strength; Right Thought is mastery; Calmness is power.

—JAMES ALLEN.
As a Man Thinketh.

The setting sun is reflected from the windows of the almshouse as brightly as from the rich man's abode; the snow melts before its door as early in the spring. I do not see but a quiet mind may live as contentedly there, and have as cheering thoughts, as in a palace.

—Henry David Thoreau.
Walden.

No one will deny that austerity is better than luxury for the spiritual life; but perfect detachment of the will and senses can be achieved without resort to merely physical expedients by those living normally in the world, and this is the essential thing. The true asceticism is a gymnastic not of the body, but of the mind. It involves training in the art of recollection; the concentration of thought, will, and love upon the eternal realities which we commonly ignore.

—Evelyn Underhill.
"The Essentials of Mysticism." *The Essentials of Mysticism and Other Essays.*

There is in connection with the thought forces what we may term, the drawing power of mind, and the great law operating here is one with that great law of the universe, that like attracts like. We are continually attracting to us from both the seen and the unseen side of life, forces and conditions most akin to those of our own thoughts.

—Ralph Waldo Trine.
In Tune with the Infinite.

It is the Thought of man; the true thaumaturgic virtue; by which man works all things whatsoever. All that he does, and brings to pass, is the vesture of a Thought. This London City, with all its houses, palaces, steam-engines, cathedrals, and huge immeasurable traffic and tumult, what is it but a Thought, but millions of Thoughts made into One;—a huge immeasurable Spirit of a THOUGHT, embodied in brick, in iron, smoke, dust, Palaces, Parliaments, Hackney Coaches, Katherine Docks, and the rest of it! Not a brick was made but some man had to think of the making of that brick.— The thing we called "bits of paper with traces of black ink," is the purest embodiment a Thought of man can have. No wonder it is, in all ways, the activest and noblest.

—Thomas Carlyle.
"The Hero as Man of Letters." *On Heroes, Hero-worship and the Heroic in History.*

Better is it when the stream of outward and inner life are both full and broad—when the glories of the material universe attract the gaze, the realm of literature and learning invite the willing feet to wander in paths where poetry has planted many flowers, philosophy many a sturdy oak of truth, which centuries cannot overthrow—and when, on the other hand, men do not forget to retire often within, and find their own minds kingdoms, where many a noble thought spontaneously grows; their own souls heavens, where, the busy world withdrawn, they commune much with their own aspirations, fight many a noble battle with whatever hinders their spiritual peace.

—Arthur Buckminster Fuller.
"Preface." *Life Without and Life Within, Or, Reviews, Narratives, Essays, and Poems* by Margaret Fuller.

Still, on itself, let Mind its eye direct,
To view the elements of intellect—
How wild Invention (daring artist!) plies
Her magic pencil, and creating dies;
And Judgment, near the living canvass, stands,
To blend the colours for her airy hands;
While Memory waits, with twilight mists o'ercast,
To mete the length'ning shadows of the past:
And bold Association, not untaught,
The links of fact, unites, with links of thought;
Forming th' electric chains, which mystic, bind
Scholastic learning, and reflective mind.

—Elizabeth Barrett Browning.
"An Essay on Mind." *An Essay on Mind, with Other Poems.*

—in all things our concern being to know and ameliorate whatever affects our inner life. Seek then to find out in the history of men what is and what is not true; in politics, what is and what is not useful; in morals, what is and what is not just; in literature, what is and what is not beautiful; in religious matters, what is and what is not pious;—in all things, what ennobles and what debases.

—Joseph Joubert.
"Of Public and Private Manners." *Pensées of Joubert.*

The mind should be empty of prejudice; when it is empty, reason comes in and dwells there. The mind should be occupied by reason; when it is occupied, passion and desire never find their way to it.

—HUNG YING-MING.
Musings of a Chinese Vegetarian.

Seek no more abroad, say I,
House and Home, but turn thine eye
Inward, and observe thy breast;
There alone dwells solid rest.
That's a close immurèd tower
Which can mock all hostile power.
To thyself a tenant be,
And inhabit safe and free.
Say not that this house is small,
Girt up in a narrow wall;
In a cleanly sober mind
Heaven itself full room doth find.

—JOSEPH BEAUMONT.
"The House of the Mind."

Intellectual achievements are the result of thought consecrated to the search for knowledge, or for the beautiful and true in life and nature.

Spiritual achievements are the consummation of holy aspirations. He who lives constantly in the conception of noble and lofty thoughts, who dwells upon all that is pure and unselfish, will, as surely as the sun reaches its zenith and the moon its full, become wise and noble in character, and rise into a position of influence and blessedness.

Achievement, of whatever kind, is the crown of effort, the diadem of thought.

—James Allen.
As a Man Thinketh.

At Learning's fountain it is sweet to drink,
But 't is a nobler privilege to think;
And oft, from books apart, the thirsting mind
May make the nectar which it cannot find.
'T is well to borrow from the good and great;
'T is wise to learn; 't is godlike to create!

—John Godfrey Saxe.
"The Library." *The Poems of John Godfrey Saxe.*

As rain breaks through an ill-thatched house, passion will break through an unreflecting mind.

As rain does not break through a well-thatched house, passion will not break through a well-reflecting mind.

—The Dhammapada.

There is a world where the active mind
Soars, unrestrained by the grovelling strife
That would press it down, and in its pinions bind
To the dull and plodding things of life.
This world is the boundless world of thought;
Where it plays, like a meteor through the sky,
And brings the forms, by its fancy caught,
To the nearer gaze of the curious eye.

But many loiter along the streams,
And quail ere the journey is begun;
Content to catch but the feeble beams
That flow from the distant central sun.
Rouse up, faint heart, from thy soft repose;
The sensual clogs from thy soul unbind;
And thy journey onward will soon disclose
A higher bliss in the world of mind.

—DAVID BATES.
"The World of Mind." *The Eolian.*

Chapter 2

On the Inner Journey, the Spiritual Path, the Spiritual Quest

First, the self is "inclined to learn true wisdom." It awakes to new needs, is cured of its belief in sham values, and distinguishes between real and unreal objects of desire. That craving for more life and more love which lies at the very heart of our selfhood, here slips from the charmed circle of the senses into a wider air.

"The first beginning of all things is a craving," says Boehme; "we are creatures of will and desire." The divine discontent, the hunger for reality, the unwillingness to be satisfied with the purely animal or the purely social level of consciousness, is the first essential stage in the development of the mystical consciousness.

—Evelyn Underhill.
"The Essentials of Mysticism." *The Essentials of Mysticism and Other Essays.*

LORD BUDDHA, *on thy lotus-throne,*
With praying eyes and hands elate,
What mystic rapture dost thou own,

Immutable and ultimate?
What peace, unravished of our ken,
Annihilate from the world of men?

The wind of change for ever blows
Across the tumult of our way,
To-morrow's unborn griefs depose
The sorrows of our yesterday.
Dream yields to dream, strife follows strife,
And Death unweaves the webs of Life.

With futile hands we seek to gain
Our inaccessible desire,
Diviner summits to attain,
With faith that sinks and feet that tire
But nought shall conquer or control
The heavenward hunger of our soul.

The end, elusive and afar,
Still lures us with its beckoning flight,
And all our mortal moments are
A session of the Infinite.
How shall we reach the great, unknown
Nirvana of thy Lotus-throne?

—SAROJINI NAIDU.
"To a Buddha seated on a Lotus." *The Golden Threshold.*

Look within. Within is the fountain of good, and it will ever bubble up, if thou wilt ever dig.

—MARCUS AURELIUS.
The Meditations of Marcus Aurelius.

The claim of the mystical consciousness is to a closer reading of truth; to an apprehension of the divine unifying principle behind appearance. " The One," says Plotinus, "is present everywhere and absent only from those unable to perceive it"; and when we do perceive it we "have another life . . . attaining the aim of our existence, and our rest." To know this at first hand—not to guess, believe or accept, but to be certain—is the highest achievement of human consciousness, and the ultimate object of mysticism.

We are invited to one gradual undivided process of sublimation, penetrating ever more deeply into the reality of the Universe, to find at last "that One who is present everywhere and absent only from those who do not perceive Him." What we behold, that we are: citizens, according to our own will and desire, of the surface world of the senses, the deeper world of life, or the ultimate world of spiritual reality.

—Evelyn Underhill.
"The Essentials of Mysticism." *The Essentials of Mysticism and Other Essays.*

Wherever, Indian Prince!
Life is—of moving things, or things unmoved,
Plant or still seed—know, what is there hath grown
By bond of Matter and of Spirit: Know
He sees indeed who sees in all alike
The living, lordly Soul; the Soul Supreme,
Imperishable amid the Perishing:
For, whoso thus beholds, in every place,
In every form, the same, one, Living Life,
Doth no more wrongfulness unto himself,

But goes the highest road which brings to bliss.
Seeing, he sees, indeed, who sees that works
Are Nature's wont, for Soul to practise by
Acting, yet not the agent; sees the mass
Of separate living things—each of its kind—
Issue from One, and blend again to One:
Then hath he BRAHMA, he attains!

—The Bhagavad-Gita.

By ceaseless efforts to live the good life we maintain our moral sanity. Not from without, but from within, flow the divine waters that renew the soul.

—Felix Adler.
Life and Destiny: Or, Thoughts from the Ethical Lectures of Felix Adler.

Our true religious life begins when we discover that there is an Inner Light, not infallible but invaluable, which "lighteth every man that cometh into the world." Then we have something to steer by; and it is chiefly this, and not an anchor, that we need. The human soul, like any other noble vessel, was not built to be anchored, but to sail.

—Thomas Wentworth Higginson.
The Sympathy of Religions.

The highest is in us all. At times it flames up and we know that we are not dust but spirit, and that in fellowship with the Spiritual Life, from whom we came, is our power and our peace.

The perennial need of human life for fresh invasions of reverence and spiritual insight seems clear. No character ever comes to its fulfillment without that. "I was common clay" says a Persian proverb, "until roses were planted in me".

—Harry Emerson Fosdick.
Twelve Tests of Character.

They said: "She dwelleth in some place apart,
Immortal Truth, within whose eyes
Who looks may find the secret of the skies
And healing for life's smart."

I sought Her in loud caverns underground,—
On heights where lightnings flashed and fell;
I scaled high Heaven; I stormed the gates of Hell,
But Her I never found

Till thro' the tumults of my Quest I caught
A whisper: "Here, within thy heart,
I dwell; for I am thou: behold, thou art
The Seeker—and the Sought."

—James H. Cousins.
"The Quest."

Chapter 3

ON PHILOSOPHY

Philosophers are the tutors of mankind; if they have found out remedies for the mind, it must be our part to employ them. I cannot think of Cato, Lelius, Socrates, Plato, without veneration: their very names are sacred to me. Philosophy is the health of the mind; let us look to that health first, and in the second place to that of the body, which may be had upon easier terms; for a strong arm, a robust constitution, or the skill of procuring this, is not a philosopher's business. He does some things as a wise man, and other things as he is a man; and he may have strength of body as well as of mind; but if he runs, or casts the sledge, it were injurious to ascribe that to his wisdom which is common to the greatest of fools. He studies rather to fill his mind than his coffers; and he knows that gold and silver were mingled with dirt, until avarice or ambition parted them. His life is ordinate, fearless, equal, secure; he stands firm in all extremities, and bears the lot of his humanity with a divine temper.

It is only philosophy that makes the mind invincible, and places us out of the reach of fortune, so that all her arrows fall short of us.

—Lucius Annaeus Seneca.
"Of a Happy Life."

That is the truly philosophic mind,
Which no inferior influence can bind;
Which all endeavours to confine were vain,
Though the earth's orbit were its length of chain.
—But not that boldness which delights to break
From what our fathers taught, for license' sake,
Through all dry places wandering, still in quest,
Like lawless fiends, of some unhallowed rest;—
The love of truth is genuine, when combined
With unaffected humbleness of mind.
He values most, who feels with sense acute
His own deep interest in the grand pursuit;
Who heaven-ward spreads his undiverted wing,
Godly simplicity the moving spring.
No meaner power can regulate his flight,
Too much is staked upon his going right.
Dry, heartless speculation may succeed,
Where the sole object is to frame a creed;
The sophist's heart may suit their eager quest,
Who only aim to prove their creed the best;
But not such views his anxious search control,
Who loves the truth because he loves his soul.
Truth is but one with Heaven, in his esteem,
The sparkling spring of life's eternal stream;
And hence, with equal singleness of heart,
He traces out each less essential part:
No worldly motives can his views entice;
He parts with all to gain the pearl of price.

—Jane Taylor.
"Prejudice." *Essays in Rhyme, on Morals and Manners.*

Keep thyself then simple, good, pure, serious, free from affectation, a friend of justice, a worshipper of the gods, kind, affectionate, strenuous in all proper acts. Strive to continue to be such as philosophy wished to make thee. Reverence the gods, and help men. Short is life. There is only one fruit of this terrene life, a pious disposition and social acts.

—MARCUS AURELIUS.
The Meditations of Marcus Aurelius.

Yet turn Philosophy! with brow sublime,
Shall Science follow on the steps of Time!
As, o'er Thought's measureless depths, we bend to hear
The whispered sound, which stole on Descartes' ear,
Hallowing the sunny visions of his youth
With that eternal mandate, "Search for Truth!"
Yes! search for Truth—the glorious path is free;
Mind shews her dwelling—Nature holds the key—
Yes! search for Truth—her tongue shall bid thee scan
The book of knowledge, for the use of Man!

—ELIZABETH BARRETT BROWNING.
"An Essay on Mind." *An Essay on Mind, with Other Poems.*

The two philosophies, that which treats of body and that which treats of mind, are both of them good, useful, and necessary. Matter must be studied by the senses and with material experience, just as mind must be studied by the inner sight, and by its own experience. Reason and imagination, patience and enthusiasm, reflection and sentiment,—

these are instruments the use of which is equally essential in our researches. To attain to truth, the soul needs all its tact and sagacity, its taste and memory, its feet and wings.

—Joseph Joubert.
"Of Philosophy." *Pensées of Joubert.*

The common condition of human society must indeed be accepted; tumult, hatred, fraud, crime, the ferocity of self-interest, the tenacity of prejudice, are perennial; but the philosopher sighs over it; his heart is not in it; his ambition is to see human history from a height; his ear is set to catch the music of the eternal spheres.

—Henri-Frédéric Amiel.
Amiel's Journal. The Journal Intime of Henri-Frédéric Amiel.

Philosophy consists not
In airy schemes, or idle speculations:
The rule and conduct of all social life
Is her great province.

—James Thomson.
Coriolanus: A Tragedy.

Chapter 4

On Wisdom

Who are the Wise?
They who have governed with a self-controul,
Each wild and baneful passion of the soul;
Curbed the strong impulse of all fierce desires,
But kept alive affection's purer fires;
They who have passed the labyrinth of life,
Without one hour of weakness or of strife;
Prepared each change of fortune to endure,
Humble though rich, and dignified though poor;
Skilled in the latent movements of the heart—
Learned in that lore which Nature can impart;
Teaching that sweet philosophy aloud,
Which sees the "silver lining" of the cloud;
Looking for good in all beneath the skies:—
These are the truly Wise!

—JOHN CRITCHLEY PRINCE.
"Who Are the Free!" *Hours with the Muses.*

Wisdom is a right understanding, a faculty of discerning good from evil; what is to be chosen, and what rejected; a judgment grounded upon the value of things, and not the common opinion of them; an equality of force, and a strength of resolution. It sets a watch over our words and deeds, it takes us up with the contemplation of the works of nature, and makes us invincible by either good or evil fortune.

—Lucius Annaeus Seneca.
"Of a Happy Life."

xcii Transcendant Wisdom.

I mean in everything. The first and highest rule of all deed and speech, the more necessary to be followed the higher and more numerous our posts, is: an ounce of wisdom is worth more than tons of cleverness. It is the only sure way, though it may not gain so much applause. The reputation of wisdom is the last triumph of fame. It is enough if you satisfy the wise, for their judgment is the touchstone of true success.

—Baltasar Gracián.
The Art of Worldly Wisdom.

Up, 'tis no dreaming-time! awake! awake!
For He who sits on the High Judge's seat
Doth in his record note each wasted hour,
Each idle word. Take heed thy shrinking soul
Find not their weight too heavy when it stands
At that dread bar from whence is no appeal.
For while we trifle the light sand steals on,
Leaving the hour-glass empty. So thy life
Glideth away. Stamp wisdom on its hours.

—Lydia Howard Sigourney.
"True Wisdom". *Pocahontas, and Other Poems.*

Wisdom is the principal thing; therefore get wisdom: and with all thy getting get understanding.

Exalt her, and she shall promote thee: she shall bring thee to honour, when thou dost embrace her.

—Proverbs 4:7-8. *KJV.*

A fourth token of the higher life is Wisdom. Wisdom is situated at the junction of the intellectual and the moral faculties. It consists in the highest use of the intellect for the discernment of the largest moral interests of humanity. It is the most perfect willingness to do the right combined with the utmost attainable knowledge of what is right, and with the clearest perception of what, in a given situation, is feasible. Wisdom is the attribute of one who works toward the most sublime ends imaginable, but who at the same time realises the limitations due to existing conditions and who, free from impatience at the unavoidable imperfections of man's estate, seeks to achieve the better as a step leading in the direction of the best.

—Felix Adler.
Life and Destiny: Or, Thoughts from the Ethical Lectures of Felix Adler.

Wisdom is a science by means of which we discern what things are and what are not good for the soul. It is the science of sciences, for it alone can estimate true value, just worth, right practice, what is dangerous and what useful.

—Joseph Joubert.
"Of Wisdom, Virtue, and Morality." *Pensées of Joubert.*

What is wisdom? That sovereign word, as has often been pointed out, is used for two different things. It may stand for knowledge, learning, science, systematic reasoning; or it may mean, as Coleridge has defined it, common sense in an uncommon degree; that is to say, the unsystematic truths that come to shrewd, penetrating, and observant minds, from their own experience of life and their daily commerce with the world, and that is called the wisdom of life, or the wisdom of the world, or the wisdom of time and the ages.

—JOHN MORLEY.
Aphorisms—an address delivered before the Edinburgh Philosophical Institution, November 11, 1887.

Not FORTUNE'S gem, AMBITION'S plume,
Nor CYTHEREA'S fading bloom,
Be objects of my pray'r:
Let av'rice, vanity, and pride,
These glitt'ring envy'd toys, divide
The dull rewards of care.

To me thy better gifts impart,
Each moral beauty of the heart
By studious thought refin'd:
For wealth, the smiles of glad content,
For pow'r, it's amplest, best extent,
An empire o'er my mind.

When fortune drops her gay parade,
When pleasure's transient roses fade,
And wither in the tomb;
Unchang'd is thy immortal prize,

Thy ever-verdant laurels rise
In undecaying bloom.

Thy breath inspires the poet's song,
The patriot's free, unbiass'd tongue,
The hero's gen'rous strife:
Thine are retirement's silent joys,
And all the sweet endearing ties
Of still, domestic life.

No more to fabled names confin'd,
To Thee! supreme, all-perfect Mind,
My thoughts direct their flight:
WISDOM'S thy gift, and all her force
From Thee deriv'd, unchanging source
Of intellectual light!

O send her sure, her steady, ray,
To regulate my doubtful way,
Thro' life's perplexing road:
The mists of error to controul,
And thro' it's gloom direct my soul
To happiness and good.

—Elizabeth Carter.
"Ode to Wisdom."

Prudence is the combination of wisdom, reason, discretion, and common sense; the offspring of a clear head, a correct judgment, and a good heart. It regards the past, the present, and the future; time and eternity; never shrinks from known duty; acts with coolness and decision; investigates impartially, reasons correctly, and condemns reluctantly.

—L. Carroll Judson.
"Prudence." The Moral Probe or One Hundred and Two Essays on the Nature of Men and Things.

The whole secret of remaining young in spite of years, and even of gray hairs, is to cherish enthusiasm in one's self by poetry, by contemplation, by charity—that is, in fewer words, by the maintenance of harmony in the soul. When everything is in its right place within us, we ourselves are in equilibrium with the whole work of God. Deep and grave enthusiasm for the eternal beauty and the eternal order, reason touched with emotion and a serene tenderness of heart—these surely are the foundations of wisdom.

Wisdom! how inexhaustible a theme! A sort of peaceful aureole surrounds and illumines this thought, in which are summed up all the treasures of moral experience, and which is the ripest fruit of a well-spent life. Wisdom never grows old, for she is the expression of order itself—that is, of the Eternal.

—Henri-Frédéric Amiel.
Amiel's Journal. The Journal Intime of Henri-Frédéric Amiel.

Knowledge and wisdom, far from being one,
Have ofttimes no connection. Knowledge dwells
In heads replete with thoughts of other men;
Wisdom in minds attentive to their own.
Knowledge, a rude unprofitable mass,

The mere materials with which wisdom builds,
Till smoothed and squared and fitted to its place,
Does but encumber whom it seems to enrich.
Knowledge is proud that he has learned so much,
Wisdom is humble that he knows no more.

—WILLIAM COWPER.
"The Task." *The Task and Other Poems.*

Chapter 5

ON PRAYER, MEDITATION, REFLECTION

And this prayer I make,
Knowing that Nature never did betray
The heart that loved her; 'tis her privilege,
Through all the years of this our life, to lead
From joy to joy: for she can so inform
The mind that is within us, so impress
With quietness and beauty, and so feed
With lofty thoughts, that neither evil tongues,
Rash judgments, nor the sneers of selfish men,
Nor greetings where no kindness is, nor all
The dreary intercourse of daily life,
Shall e'er prevail against us, or disturb
Our cheerful faith that all which we behold
Is full of blessings. Therefore let the moon
Shine on thee in thy solitary walk;
And let the misty mountain winds be free
To blow against thee: and in after years,
When these wild ecstasies shall be matured
Into a sober pleasure, when thy mind
Shall be a mansion for all lovely forms,
Thy memory be as a dwelling-place
For all sweet sounds and harmonies; Oh! then,

If solitude, or fear, or pain, or grief,
Should be thy portion, with what healing thoughts
Of tender joy wilt thou remember me,
And these my exhortations!

—WILLIAM WORDSWORTH.
"Lines Written a Few Miles Above Tintern Abbey."
Lyrical Ballads, with a Few Other Poems.

Prayer that craves a particular commodity, any thing less than all good, is vicious. Prayer is the contemplation of the facts of life from the highest point of view. It is the soliloquy of a beholding and jubilant soul. It is the spirit of God pronouncing his works good. But prayer as a means to effect a private end is meanness and theft. It supposes dualism and not unity in nature and consciousness. As soon as the man is at one with God, he will not beg. He will then see prayer in all action.

—RALPH WALDO EMERSON.
"Self-Reliance." *Essays, First Series.*

Prayer is the soul's sincere desire,
Uttered or unexpressed—
The motion of a hidden fire
That trembles in the breast.

Prayer is the burthen of a sigh,
The falling of a tear—
The upward glancing of an eye,
When none but God is near.

*Prayer is the simplest form of speech
That infant lips can try—
Prayer the sublimest strains that reach
The majesty on high.*

—JAMES MONTGOMERY.
"Prayer is the Soul's Sincere Desire." *A Church of
England Hymn Book.*

*Who truth pursues, who from false ways
His heedful steps would keep,
By inward light must search within
In meditation deep;
All outward bent he must repress
His soul's true treasure to possess.*

—BOETHIUS.
"Book III. Song XI." *The Consolation of Philosophy of Boethius.*

*I do not ask for any crown
But that which all may win
Nor seek to conquer any world
Except the one within.
Be thou my guide until I find,
Led by a tender hand,
Thy happy kingdom in myself
And dare to take command.*

—LOUISA MAY ALCOTT.
"My Kingdom."

But the beauty which we seek to incorporate into our spiritual intercourse should not be the dead ceremonious beauty which comes of mere dependence on tradition. It should be the freely upspringing lyric beauty which is rooted in intense personal feeling; the living beauty of a living thing. Nor need we fear the reproach that here we confuse religion with poetry. Poetry ever goes like the royal banners before ascending life; therefore man may safely follow its leadership in his prayer, which is—or should be—life in its intensest form.

The springs of the truest prayer and of the deepest poetry—twin expressions of man's outward-going passion for that Eternity which is his home—rise very near together in the heart.

—EVELYN UNDERHILL.
"The Place of Will, Intellect, and Feeling in Prayer."
The Essentials of Mysticism and Other Essays.

The harp at Nature's advent strung
    Has never ceased to play;
The song the stars of morning sung
    Has never died away.

And prayer is made, and praise is given,
    By all things near and far;
The ocean looketh up to heaven,
    And mirrors every star.

Its waves are kneeling on the strand,
    As kneels the human knee,

Their white locks bowing to the sand,
    The priesthood of the sea!

They pour their glittering treasures forth,
    Their gifts of pearl they bring,
And all the listening hills of earth
    Take up the song they sing.

The green earth sends its incense up
    From many a mountain shrine;
From folded leaf and dewy cup
    She pours her sacred wine.

The mists above the morning rills
    Rise white as wings of prayer;
The altar-curtains of the hills
    Are sunset's purple air.

The winds with hymns of praise are loud,
    Or low with sobs of pain,—
The thunder-organ of the cloud,
    The dropping tears of rain.

With drooping head and branches crossed
    The twilight forest grieves,
Or speaks with tongues of Pentecost
    From all its sunlit leaves.

The blue sky is the temple's arch,
    Its transept earth and air,
The music of its starry march
    The chorus of a prayer.

So Nature keeps the reverent frame
  With which her years began,
And all her signs and voices shame
  The prayerless heart of man.

—JOHN GREENLEAF WHITTIER.
"The Worship of Nature." *The Complete Poetical Works of Whittier.*

Let me to-day do something that shall take
  A little sadness from the world's vast store,
And may I be so favoured as to make
  Of joy's too scanty sum a little more.
Let me not hurt, by any selfish deed
  Or thoughtless word, the heart of foe or friend;
Nor would I pass, unseeing, worthy need,
  Or sin by silence when I should defend.
However meagre be my worldly wealth,
  Let me give something that shall aid my kind,
A word of courage, or a thought of health,
  Dropped as I pass for troubled hearts to find.
Let me to-night look back across the span
  'Twixt dawn and dark, and to my conscience say—
Because of some good act to beast or man—
  "The world is better that I lived to-day."

—ELLA WHEELER WILCOX.
"Morning Prayer." *Poems of Power.*

...Prayer is the peace of our spirit, the stillness of our thoughts, the evenness of recollection, the seat of meditation, the rest of our cares, and the calm of our tempest; prayer is the issue of a quiet mind, of untroubled thoughts, it is the daughter of charity, and the sister of meekness....

—Jeremy Taylor.
"Sermon V." *Discourses on Various Subjects, Volume 1.*

And let thy favour, to the end of life,
Inspire me with ability to seek
Repose and hope among eternal things—
Father of heaven and earth! and I am rich,
And will possess my portion in content!

—William Wordsworth.
"Book Fourth. Despondency Corrected." *The Excursion.*

Thou that canst still the raging of the seas,
Chain up the winds, and bid the tempests cease,
Redeem my shipwreck'd soul from raging gusts
Of cruel passion and deceitful lusts;
From storms of rage and dangerous rocks of pride,
Let thy strong hand this little vessel guide,
(It was thy hand that made it) through the tide
Impetuous of this life, let thy command
Direct my course, and bring me safe to land.

—Matthew Prior.
Solomon On The Vanity Of The World,
A Poem. In Three Books.

We have always need of the infinite, the eternal, the absolute; and since science contents itself with what is relative, it necessarily leaves a void, which it is good for man to fill with contemplation, worship, and adoration. "Religion," said Bacon, "is the spice which is meant to keep life from corruption," and this is especially true to-day of religion taken in the Platonist and oriental sense. A capacity for self-recollection—for withdrawal from the outward to the inward—is in fact the condition of all noble and useful activity.

—Henri-Frédéric Amiel.
Amiel's Journal: The Journal Intime of Henri-Frédéric Amiel.

As in the silence of the night, the ear catches the least sound; so, in the solitude of reflection, the mind detects soft and delicate strains of thought, unheard in the bustle of the crowd.

—Prentice Mulford.
"Coarse Gold."

Chapter 6

On Conscience, the Inner Voice

Man cannot get away from facts—
Alas, stern duty looms supreme,
For certain things we must perform,
Obey the inward voices' call.
Calm joyous days cannot be wooed
Unless our conscience is at peace.

—Sadakichi Hartmann.
My Rubaiyat.

Listen to the gentle monitor within; a good conscience is a safe counsellor, and to follow it is to steer in a right direction.

—Ida Scott Taylor.
"January Thirteenth." *The Year Book of English Authors.*

Even in the fiercest uproar of our stormy passions, Conscience, though in her softest whispers, gives to the supremacy of rectitude the voice of an undying testimony; and her light still shining in a dark place, her unquelled accents still heard in the loudest outcry of Nature's rebellious appetites, form the strongest argument within reach of the human faculties, that, in spite of all partial of temporary derangements, Supreme Power and Supreme Goodness are at one.

—Dr. Thomas Chalmers.
"The Supremacy of Conscience." *On Natural Theology. Volume 1.*

"Good-bye," I said to my conscience—
"Good-bye for aye and aye,"
And I put her hands off harshly,
And turned my face away;
And conscience smitten sorely
Returned not from that day.

But a time came when my spirit
Grew weary of its pace;
And I cried: "Come back, my conscience;
I long to see thy face."
But conscience cried: "I cannot;
Remorse sits in my place."

—Paul Laurence Dunbar.
"Conscience and Remorse." *Lyrics of Lowly Life.*

Look within. Within is the fountain of good, and it will ever bubble up, if thou wilt ever dig.

—Marcus Aurelius.
The Meditations of Marcus Aurelius..

The authority of conscience is founded on human nature itself. The imperative, which we cannot disown, comes from within. The distinction between right and wrong is as aboriginal as that between the true and the false.

—Felix Adler.
Life and Destiny: Or, Thoughts from the Ethical Lectures of Felix Adler.

Be humble, devout, silent, that so thou mayest hear within the depths of thyself the subtle and profound voice; be spiritual and pure, that so thou mayest have communion with the pure spirit. Withdraw thyself often into the sanctuary of thy inmost consciousness; become once more point and atom, that so thou mayest free thyself from space, time, matter, temptation, dispersion....

—Henri-Frédéric Amiel.
Amiel's Journal: The Journal Intime of Henri-Frédéric Amiel.

A good conscience is to the soul what health is to the body; it preserves constant ease and serenity within us; and more than countervails all the calamities and afflictions which can befall us from without.

—Joseph Addison.
The Works of the Right Honourable Joseph Addison, Volume IV.

Our only talisman lies in that concentration of moral force which we call conscience, that small inextinguishable flame of which the light is duty and the warmth love. This little flame should be the star of our life; it alone can guide our trembling ark across the tumult of the great waters; it alone can enable us to escape the temptations of the sea, the storms and the monsters which are the offspring of night and the deluge.

—Henri-Frédéric Amiel.
Amiel's Journal: The Journal Intime of Henri-Frédéric Amiel.

But, above all, the victory is most sure
For him, who, seeking faith by virtue, strives
To yield entire submission to the law
Of conscience—conscience reverenced and obeyed,
As God's most intimate presence in the soul,
And his most perfect image in the world.

—William Wordsworth.
"Book Fourth. Despondency Corrected." *The Excursion.*

Have a good conscience and thou shalt ever have joy. A good conscience is able to bear exceeding much, and is exceeding joyful in the midst of adversities; an evil conscience is ever fearful and unquiet. Thou shalt rest sweetly if thy heart condemn thee not. Never rejoice unless when thou hast done well.

—Thomas à Kempis.
"Second Book." *The Imitation of Christ.*

But self-control, this truest and greatest monarchy, rarely comes by inheritance. Every one of us must conquer himself; and we may do so, if we take conscience for our guide and general.

—Sir John Lubbock.
"The Happiness of Duty." *The Pleasures of Life, Part I and Part II.*

The voice of conscience speaks in duty done; and without its regulating and controlling influence, the brightest and greatest intellect may be merely as a light that leads astray. Conscience sets a man upon his feet, while his will holds him upright. Conscience is the moral governor of the heart—the governor of right action, of right thought, of right faith, of right life—and only through its dominating influence can the noble and upright character be fully developed.

—Samuel Smiles.
"Chapter VII. Duty—Truthfulness." *Character.*

Conscience, as the mentor, the guide and compass of every act, leads ever to Happiness. When the individual can stay alone with his conscience and get its approval, without using force or specious logic, then he begins to know what real Happiness is.

He can shut his ears to "what the world says" and find in the approval of his own conscience the highest earthly tribune,—the voice of the Infinite communing with the Individual.

—William George Jordan.
The Majesty of Calmness.

At first religion holds the place of science and philosophy; afterward she has to learn to confine herself to her own domain—which is in the inmost depths of conscience, in the secret recesses of the soul, where life communes with the Divine will and the universal order. Piety is the daily renewing of the ideal, the steadying of our inner being, agitated, troubled, and embittered by the common accidents of existence. Prayer is the spiritual balm, the precious cordial which restores to us peace and courage. It reminds us of pardon and of duty. It says to us, "Thou art loved—love; thou hast received—give; thou must die—labor while thou canst; overcome anger by kindness; overcome evil with good.......... Thou hast a witness in thy conscience; and thy conscience is God speaking to thee!"

—Henri-Frédéric Amiel.
Amiel's Journal: The Journal Intime of Henri-Frédéric Amiel.

Knowledge or wealth to few are given,
But, mark, how just the ways of Heaven!
True joy to all is free:
Nor wealth, nor knowledge, grant the boon;
'Tis thine, O Conscience! thine alone,
It all belongs to thee.

—William Julius Mickle.
"Knowledge: An Ode." *The Poetical Works of William Julius Mickle.*

Part Two

ON THE NATURE
OF THINGS

Chapter 7

On the Lessons of Nature

How countless and how multiform the scenes
Nature presents, expanding as we tread
Her sacred precincts! With what various tongues
She teaches, and how vast the wisdom gained!

Nature is man's best teacher. She unfolds
Her treasures to his search, unseals his eye,
Illumes his mind, and purifies his heart.
An influence breathes from all the sights and sounds
Of her existence; she is Wisdom's self.
Rest yields she to the "weary" of the earth—
Its "heavy-laden" she endows with strength.

—Alfred Billings Street.
"Nature." *The Poems of Alfred B. Street.*

The human mind, actively occupied, is apt to go astray. When we sit down quietly, with no idea to agitate the mind, we can commune with nature. If we see a cloud appearing on the horizon, we shall follow it in its wandering in the blue. If we hear rain dripping from the eaves, we shall feel our bosoms cooled and purified. If we listen to birds singing, we shall be cheered up by their songs. If we see flowers falling, we shall know that anything flourishing cannot last long. Thus, when we are in communion with nature, what spot or what object is there that does not teach us something about the truth?

—HUNG YING-MING.
Musings of a Chinese Vegetarian.

The harp at Nature's advent strung
Has never ceased to play;
The song the stars of morning sung
Has never died away.
And prayer is made, and praise is given,
By all things near and far;
The ocean looketh up to heaven,
And mirrors every star.
Its waves are kneeling on the strand,
As kneels the human knee,
Their white locks bowing to the sand,
The priesthood of the sea!
They pour their glittering treasures forth,
Their gifts of pearl they bring,
And all the listening hills of earth
Take up the song they sing.
The green earth sends its incense up
From many a mountain shrine;
From folded leaf and dewy cup
She pours her sacred wine.
The mists above the morning rills
Rise white as wings of prayer;
The altar-curtains of the hills
Are sunset's purple air.

The winds with hymns of praise are loud,
Or low with sobs of pain,—
The thunder-organ of the cloud,
The dropping tears of rain.
With drooping head and branches crossed
The twilight forest grieves,
Or speaks with tongues of Pentecost
From all its sunlit leaves.
The blue sky is the temple's arch,
Its transept earth and air,
The music of its starry march
The chorus of a prayer.
So Nature keeps the reverent frame
With which her years began,
And all her signs and voices shame
The prayerless heart of man.

—JOHN GREENLEAF WHITTIER.
"The Worship of Nature." *The Complete Poetical Works of Whittier.*

It seems as if the day was not wholly profane in which we have given heed to some natural object. The fall of snowflakes in a still air, preserving to each crystal its perfect form; the blowing of sleet over a wide sheet of water, and over plains; the waving ryefield; the mimic waving of acres of houstonia, whose innumerable florets whiten and ripple before the eye; the reflections of trees and flowers in glassy lakes; the musical steaming odorous south wind, which converts all trees to windharps; the crackling and spurting of hemlock in the flames, or of pine logs, which yield glory to the walls and faces in the sittingroom,—these are the music and pictures of the most ancient religion.

—Ralph Waldo Emerson.
"Nature." *Essays, Second Series.*

"And this our life, exempt from public haunt, finds tongues in trees, books in the running brooks, sermons in stones, and good in everything. I would not change it."

—William Shakespeare.
As You Like It.

For I have learned
To look on nature, not as in the hour
Of thoughtless youth, but hearing oftentimes
The still, sad music of humanity,
Nor harsh nor grating, though of ample power
To chasten and subdue. And I have felt
A presence that disturbs me with the joy
Of elevated thoughts; a sense sublime
Of something far more deeply interfused,
Whose dwelling is the light of setting suns,
And the round ocean, and the living air,
And the blue sky, and in the mind of man,
A motion and a spirit, that impels
All thinking things, all objects of all thought,
And rolls through all things. Therefore am I still
A lover of the meadows and the woods,
And mountains; and of all that we behold

From this green earth; of all the mighty world
Of eye and ear, both what they half-create,
And what perceive; well pleased to recognize
In nature and the language of the sense,
The anchor of my purest thoughts, the nurse,
The guide, the guardian of my heart, and soul
Of all my moral being.

—William Wordsworth.
"Lines Written a Few Miles Above Tintern Abbey."
Lyrical Ballads, with a Few Other Poems.

When the moon shines brightly on the snow-covered earth, the mind naturally feels calm and purified. The genial breeze of spring, rendering the air sweet and crisp, softens our hearts into serenity. Potent is the influence of nature over the human mind, and this proves that there exists a sympathy between nature and man.

—Hung Ying-Ming.
Musings of a Chinese Vegetarian.

Art is the child of Nature; yes,
Her darling child, in whom we trace
The features of the mother's face,
Her aspect and her attitude,
All her majestic loveliness
Chastened and softened and subdued
Into a more attractive grace,
And with a human sense imbued.
He is the greatest artist, then,

Whether of pencil or of pen,
Who follows Nature. Never man,
As artist or as artisan,
Pursuing his own fantasies,
Can touch the human heart, or please,
Or satisfy our nobler needs,
As he who sets his willing feet
In Nature's footprints, light and fleet,
And follows fearless where she leads.

—HENRY WADSWORTH LONGFELLOW.
"Keramos." *Keramos and Other Poems.*

Till the rain comes they take no heed whatever, but then make for shelter. Blackbirds often make a good deal of noise; but the soft turtle-doves coo gently, let the lightning be as savage as it will. Nothing has the least fear. Man alone, more senseless than a pigeon, put a god in vapour; and to this day, though the printing press has set a foot on every threshold, numbers bow the knee when they hear the roar the timid dove does not heed. So trustful are the doves, the squirrels, the birds of the branches, and the creatures of the field. Under their tuition let us rid ourselves of mental terrors, and face death itself as calmly as they do the livid lightning; so trustful and so content with their fate, resting in themselves and unappalled. If but by reason and will I could reach the godlike calm and courage of what we so thoughtlessly call the timid turtle-dove, I should lead a nearly perfect life.

—RICHARD JEFFERIES.
The Pageant of Summer.

Remote from cities liv'd a swain,
Unvex'd with all the cares of gain;
His head was silver'd o'er with age,
And long experience made him sage;
In summer's heat and winter's cold,
He led his flock and penn'd the fold;
His hours in cheerful labour flew,
Nor envy nor ambition knew:
His wisdom and his honest fame
Through all the country rais'd his name.

A deep philosopher (whose rules
Of moral life were drawn from schools)
The shepherd's homely cottage sought,
And thus explor'd his reach of thought.

'Whence is thy learning? Hath thy toil
O'er books consum'd the midnight oil?
Hast thou old Greece and Rome survey'd,
And the vast sense of Plato weigh'd?

The shepherd modestly replied,
'I ne'er the paths of learning tried;
Nor have I roam'd in foreign parts,
To read mankind, their laws and arts;

The little knowledge I have gain'd,
Was all from simple nature drain'd;
Hence my life's maxims took their rise,
Hence grew my settled hate to vice.
The daily labours of the bee
Awake my soul to industry.
Who can observe the careful ant,

And not provide for future want?
'From nature too I take my rule,
To shun contempt and ridicule.
I never, with important air,
In conversation overbear.
Can grave and formal pass for wise,
When men the solemn owl despise?
My tongue within my lips I rein;
For who talks much must talk in vain,
We from the wordy torrent fly:
Who listens to the chatt'ring pye?

Thus ev'ry object of creation
Can furnish hints to contemplation;
And from the most minute and mean,
A virtuous mind can morals glean.'

'Thy fame is just,' the sage replies;
'Thy virtue proves thee truly wise.
Pride often guides the author's pen,
Books as affected are as men:
But he who studies nature's laws,
From certain truth his maxims draws;
And those, without our schools, suffice,
To make men moral, good, and wise.'

—JOHN GAY.
"The Shepherd and the Philosopher." *The Poetical Works of John Gay.*

Every flower that gives its fragrance to the wandering air, leaves its influence on the soul of man. The wheel and swoop of the winged creatures of the air suggest the flowing lines of subtle art. The roar and murmur of the restless sea, the cataract's solemn chant, the thunder's voice, the happy babble of the brook, the whispering leaves, the thrilling notes of mating birds, the sighing winds, taught man to pour his heart in song, and gave a voice to grief and hope, to love and death.

—ROBERT GREEN INGERSOLL.
"Nature." *The Philosophy of Ingersoll.*

How the might of Nature sways
All the world in ordered ways,
How resistless laws control
Each least portion of the whole.

—BOETHIUS.
"Book III. Song II." *The Consolation of Philosophy of Boethius.*

The exceeding beauty of the earth, in her splendour of life, yields a new thought with every petal. The hours when the mind is absorbed by beauty are the only hours when we really live, so that the longer we can stay among these things so much the more is snatched from inevitable Time. Let the shadow advance upon the dial—I can watch it with equanimity while it is there to be watched. It is only when the shadow is *not* there, when the clouds of winter cover it, that the dial is terrible. The invisible shadow goes on and steals from us. But now, while I can see the shadow of the tree and watch it slowly gliding along the surface of the grass, it is mine. These are the only hours that are not wasted—these hours that absorb the soul and fill it with beauty. This is real life, and all else is illusion, or mere endurance. Does this reverie of flowers and waterfall and song form an ideal, a human ideal, in the mind? It does; much the same ideal that Phidias sculptured of man and woman filled with a godlike sense of the violet fields of Greece, beautiful beyond thought, calm as my turtle-dove before the lurid lightning of the unknown. To be beautiful and to be calm, without mental fear, is the ideal of nature. If I cannot achieve it, at least I can think it.

—RICHARD JEFFERIES.
The Pageant of Summer.

And hark! how blithe the throstle sings!
He, too, is no mean preacher:
Come forth into the light of things,
Let Nature be your teacher.

She has a world of ready wealth,
Our minds and hearts to bless—
Spontaneous wisdom breathed by health,
Truth breathed by cheerfulness.

One impulse from a vernal wood
May teach you more of man,
Of moral evil and of good,
Than all the sages can.

Sweet is the lore which Nature brings;
Our meddling intellect
Mis-shapes the beauteous forms of things:—
We murder to dissect.

Enough of Science and of Art;
Close up those barren leaves;
Come forth, and bring with you a heart
That watches and receives.

—WILLIAM WORDSWORTH.
"The Tables Turned." *Poems of Wordsworth.*

I cannot open my eyes without admiring the art that shines throughout all nature; the least cast suffices to make me perceive the Hand that makes everything. Nay, what is called the art of men is but a faint imitation of the great art called the laws of Nature, and which the impious did not blush to call blind chance.

—FRANCOIS DE SALIGNAC DE LA MOTHE-FÉNELON.
A Demonstration of the Existence and Attributes of God.

Nature is an aeolian harp, a musical instrument whose tones are the re-echo of higher strings within us.

—NOVALIS (GEORG PHILIPP FRIEDRICH FREIHERR VON HARDENBERG).

For the world is a most holy and divine temple, into which man is introduced at his birth, not to behold motionless images made by hands, but those things (to use the language of Plato) which the divine mind has exhibited as the visible representations of invisible things, having innate in them the principle of life and motion, as the sun moon and stars, and rivers ever flowing with fresh water, and the earth affording maintenance to plants and animals. Seeing then that life is the most complete initiation into all these things, it ought to be full of ease of mind and joy.

—P<small>LUTARCH</small>.
"On Contentedness of Mind."

If the day and the night are such that you greet them with joy, and life emits a fragrance like flowers and sweet-scented herbs, is more elastic, more starry, more immortal,—that is your success. All nature is your congratulation, and you have cause momentarily to bless yourself. The greatest gains and values are farthest from being appreciated. We easily come to doubt if they exist. We soon forget them. They are the highest reality. Perhaps the facts most astounding and most real are never communicated by man to man. The true harvest of my daily life is somewhat as intangible and indescribable as the tints of morning or evening. It is a little star-dust caught, a segment of the rainbow which I have clutched.

—H<small>ENRY</small> D<small>AVID</small> T<small>HOREAU</small>.
Walden.

Better for us, perhaps, it might appear,
Were there all harmony, all virtue here;
That never air or ocean felt the wind;
That never passion discomposed the mind.
But all subsists by elemental strife;
And passions are the elements of life.

The general order, since the whole began,
Is kept in nature, and is kept in man.

—ALEXANDER POPE.
"Epistle I." *An Essay on Man. Moral Essays and Satires.*

The works of God are fair for nought
Unless our eyes, in seeing,
See, hidden in the thing, the thought
That animates its being.

The outward form is not the whole,
But every part is moulded
To image forth an inward soul
That dimly is unfolded.

The stars are lighted in the skies
Not merely for their shining,
But, like the looks of loving eyes,
Have meanings worth divining.

The waves that moan along the shore,
The winds that sigh in blowing,
Are sent to teach a mystic lore
Which men are wise in knowing.

The clouds around the mountain peak,
The rivers in their winding,
Have secrets which, to all who seek,
Are precious in the finding.

Thus Nature dwells within our reach,
But, though we stand so near her,

We still interpret half her speech
With ears too dull to hear her.

Whoever, at the coarsest sound,
Still listens for the finest,
Shall hear the noisy world go round
To music the divinest.

Whoever yearns to see aright
Because his heart is tender,
Shall catch a glimpse of heavenly light
In every earthly splendor.

So, since the universe began,
And till it shall be ended,
The soul of Nature, soul of Man,
And soul of God are blended!

—THEODORE TILTON.
"The Mystery of Nature." *The Sexton's Tale, and Other Poems.*

Nature we always have with us, an inexhaustible storehouse of that which moves the heart, appeals to the mind, and fires the imagination,—health to the body, a stimulus to the intellect, and joy to the soul. To the scientist Nature is a storehouse of facts, laws, processes; to the artist she is a storehouse of pictures; to the poet she is a storehouse of images, fancies, a source of inspiration; to the moralist she is a storehouse of precepts and parables; to all she may be a source of knowledge and joy.

—JOHN BURROUGHS.
"The Art of Seeing Things." *Leaf and Tendril.*

Chapter 8

ON THE MYSTERIES OF LIFE

The mystery of life is what makes life worth living. "'Twas a little being of mystery, like every one else,' says the old King Arkel of the dead Mélisande. We are such stuff as dreams are made of, might be the 'refrain' of all M. Maeterlinck's plays, and of most of these essays. He is penetrated by the feeling of the mystery in all human creatures, whose every act is regulated by far-off influences and obscurely rooted in things unexplained. Mystery is within us and around us. Of reality we can only get now and then the merest glimpse. Our senses are too gross. Between the invisible world and our own there is doubtless an intimate concordance; but it escapes us. We grope among shadows towards the unknown. Even the new conquests of what we vainly suppose to be 'exact' thought only deepen the mystery of life.

—A. B. WALKLEY.
"Introduction". *The Treasure of the Humble*. By Maurice Maeterlinck.

Ponder on God's mercies,
But not on His essence.
For His works come forth from His essence,

Not His essence from His works.
His light shines on the whole universe,
Yet He Himself is hidden from the universe.

—MAHMUD SHABISTARI.
"Part X. The One." *The Secret Rose Garden of Sa'd Ud Din Mahmud Shabistari.*

The Creator brought into being the Game of Joy: and from the word
Om the Creation sprang.
The earth is His joy; His joy is the sky;
His joy is the flashing of the sun and the moon;
His joy is the beginning, the middle, and the end;
His joy is eyes, darkness, and light.
Oceans and waves are His joy: His joy the Sarasvati, the Jumna, and the Ganges.
The Guru is One: and life and death., union and separation, are all His plays of joy!
His play the land and water, the whole universe!
His play the earth and the sky!
In play is the Creation spread out, in play it is established.
The whole world, says Kabîr, rests in His play, yet still the Player remains unknown.

—KABIR.
Songs of Kabir.

That great mystery of Time, were there no other; the illimitable, silent, never-resting thing called Time, rolling, rushing on, swift, silent, like an all-embracing ocean-tide, on which we and all the Universe swim like exhalations, like apparitions which are, and then are not: this is forever very literally a miracle; a thing to strike us dumb,—for we have no word to speak about it. This Universe, ah me—what could the wild man know of it; what can we yet know? That it is a Force, and thousand-fold Complexity of Forces; a Force which is not we. That is all; it is not we, it is altogether different from us. Force, Force, everywhere Force; we ourselves a mysterious Force in the centre of that.

—Thomas Carlyle.
"The Hero as Divinity." *On Heroes, Hero-worship and the Heroic in History.*

This earth is but a semblance and a form—
An apparition poised in boundless space;
This life we live so sensible and warm,
Is but a dreaming in a sleep that stays
About us from the cradle to the grave.
Things seen are as inconstant as a wave
That must obey the impulse of the wind;
So in this strange communicable being
There is a higher consciousness confined—
But separate and divine, and foreseeing.

—William Stanley Braithwaite.
"The Eternal Self (to Vere Goldthwaite)." *The House of Falling Leaves With Other Poems.*

Vates means both Prophet and Poet: and indeed at all times, Prophet and Poet, well understood, have much kindred of meaning. Fundamentally indeed they are still the same; in this most important respect especially, that they have penetrated both of them into the sacred mystery of the Universe; what Goethe calls "the open secret." "Which is the great secret?" asks one.—"The open secret,"—open to all, seen by almost none! That divine mystery, which lies everywhere in all Beings, "the Divine Idea of the World, that which lies at the bottom of Appearance," as Fichte styles it; of which all Appearance, from the starry sky to the grass of the field, but especially the Appearance of Man and his work, is but the vesture, the embodiment that renders it visible. This divine mystery is in all times and in all places; veritably is.

—Thomas Carlyle.
"The Hero as Poet." *On Heroes, Hero-worship and the Heroic in History.*

The nameless is the boundary of Heaven and Earth.
The named is the mother of creation.
Freed from desire, you can see the hidden mystery.
By having desire, you can only see what is visibly real.
Yet mystery and reality emerge from the same source.

—Lao-Tzu.
Tao Te Ching.

In every religion there is an element of the supernatural, varying with the influence of pure reason over its devotees. The Indian was a logical and clear thinker upon matters within the scope of his understanding, but he had not yet charted the vast field of nature or expressed her wonders in terms of science. With his limited knowledge of cause and effect, he saw miracles on every hand,—the miracle of life in seed and egg, the miracle of death in lightning flash and in the swelling deep! Nothing of the marvelous could astonish him; as that a beast should speak, or the sun stand still. The virgin birth would appear scarcely more miraculous than is the birth of every child that comes into the world, or the miracle of the loaves and fishes excite more wonder than the harvest that springs from a single ear of corn.

Who may condemn his superstition? Surely not the devout Catholic, or even Protestant missionary, who teaches Bible miracles as literal fact! The logical man must either deny all miracles or none, and our American Indian myths and hero stories are perhaps, in themselves, quite as credible as those of the Hebrews of old. If we are of the modern type of mind, that sees in natural law a majesty and grandeur far more impressive than any solitary infraction of it could possibly be, let us not forget that, after all, science has not explained everything. We have still to face the ultimate miracle,—the origin and principle of life! Here is the supreme mystery that is the essence of worship, without which there can be no religion, and in the presence of this mystery our attitude cannot be very unlike that of the natural philosopher, who beholds with awe the Divine in all creation.

—CHARLES ALEXANDER EASTMAN (OHIYESA).
"The Great Mystery." *The Soul of the Indian: An Interpretation.*

I was not; now I am—a few days hence
I shall not be; I fain would look before
And after, but can neither do; some Power

Or lack of power says "no" to all I would.
I stand upon a wide and sunless plain,
Nor chart nor steel to guide my steps aright.
Whene'er, o'ercoming fear, I dare to move,
I grope without direction and by chance.
Some feign to hear a voice and feel a hand
That draws them ever upward thro' the gloom.
But I—I hear no voice and touch no hand,
Tho' oft thro' silence infinite I list,
And strain my hearing to supernal sounds;
Tho' oft thro' fateful darkness do I reach,
And stretch my hand to find that other hand.
I question of th' eternal bending skies
That seem to neighbor with the novice earth;
But they roll on, and daily shut their eyes
On me, as I one day shall do on them,
And tell me not the secret that I ask.

—PAUL LAURENCE DUNBAR.
"The Mystery." *Lyrics of Lowly Life.*

Human existence is girt round with mystery: the narrow region of our experience is a small island in the midst of a boundless sea, which at once awes our feelings and stimulates our imagination by its vastness and its obscurity. To add to the mystery, the domain of our earthly existence is not only an island in infinite space, but also in infinite time. The past and the future are alike shrouded from us: we neither know the origin of anything which is, nor its final destination.

—JOHN STUART MILL.
Nature, the Utility of Religion, and Theism.

We cannot kindle when we will
The fire which in the heart resides;
The spirit bloweth and is still,
In mystery our soul abides.

—MATTHEW ARNOLD.
"Morality." *Poetical Works of Matthew Arnold.*

The efficacy of religion lies precisely in that which is not rational, philosophic, nor external; its efficacy lies in the unforeseen, the miraculous, the extraordinary. Thus religion attracts more devotion in proportion as it demands more faith—that is to say, as it becomes more incredible to the profane mind. The philosopher aspires to explain away all mysteries, to dissolve them into light. It is mystery, on the other hand, which the religious instinct demands and pursues; it is mystery which constitutes the essence of worship.....

So long then as the life of nations is in need of religion as a motive and sanction of morality, as food for faith, hope, and charity, so long will the masses turn away from pure reason and naked truth, so long will they adore mystery, so long—and rightly so—will they rest in faith, the only region where the ideal presents itself to them in an attractive form.

—HENRI-FRÉDÉRIC AMIEL.
Amiel's Journal. The Journal Intime of Henri-Frédéric Amiel.

All things being are in mystery; we expound mysteries by mysteries;
And yet the secret of them all is one in simple grandeur:

All intricate, yet each path plain, to those who know the way;
All unapproachable, yet easy of access, to them that hold the key:
We walk among labyrinths of wonder, but thread the mazes with a clue;
We sail in chartless seas, but behold! the pole-star is above us.

For mystery is man's life; we wake to the whisperings of novelty:
And what, though we lie down disappointed? we sleep, to wake in hope.
The letter, or the news, the chances and the changes, matters that may happen,
Sweeten or embitter daily life with the honey-gall of mystery.

Praise God, creature of earth, for the mercies linked with secresy,
That spices of uncertainty enrich the cup of life;
Praise God, His hosts on high, for the mysteries that make all joy;
What were intelligence with nothing more to learn, or heaven, in eternity of sameness?

O Mysteries, ye all are one, the mind of an inexplicable Architect
Dwelleth alike in each, quickening and moving in them all.

—MARTIN FARQUHAR TUPPER.
"Of Mystery." *Proverbial Philosophy: A Book of Thoughts and Arguments.*

Chapter 9

ON HIGHER LAWS, UNSEEN ORDER, DIVINE ORDER

For to each thing God hath given
Its appointed time;
No perplexing change permits He
In His plan sublime.

—BOETHIUS.
"Book I. Song VI." *The Consolation of*
Philosophy of Boethius.

There is, then, this Spirit of Infinite Life and Power behind all which is the source of all. This Infinite Power is creating, working, ruling through the agency of great immutable laws and forces that run through all the universe, that surround us on every side. Every act of our every-day lives is governed by these same great laws and forces. Every flower that blooms by the wayside, springs up, grows, blooms, fades, according to certain great immutable laws. Every snowflake that plays between earth and heaven, forms, falls, melts, according to certain great unchangeable laws.

—RALPH WALDO TRINE.
In Tune with the Infinite.

Whichever way the wind doth blow,
Some heart is glad to have it so;
Then blow it east or blow it west,
The wind that blows, that wind is best.

And so I do not dare to pray
For winds to waft me on my way,
But leave it to a Higher Will
To stay or speed me; trusting still
That all is well, and sure that He
Who launched my bark will sail with me
Through storm and calm, and will not fail,
Whatever breezes may prevail,
To land me, every peril past,
Within his sheltering heaven at last.

Then, whatsoever wind doth blow,
My heart is glad to have it so;
And blow it east or blow it west,
The wind that blows, that wind is best.

—Caroline Atherton Mason.
"The Voyage."

On the whole, as this wondrous planet, Earth, is journeying with its fellows through infinite Space, so are the wondrous destinies embarked on it journeying through infinite Time, under a higher guidance than ours.

—Thomas Carlyle.
"Signs of the Time."

Cease, then, nor order imperfection name:
Our proper bliss depends on what we blame.
Know thy own point: this kind, this due degree
Of blindness, weakness, Heaven bestows on thee.
Submit. In this, or any other sphere,
Secure to be as blest as thou canst bear:
Safe in the hand of one disposing Power,
Or in the natal, or the mortal hour.
All nature is but art, unknown to thee;
All chance, direction, which thou canst not see;
All discord, harmony not understood;
All partial evil, universal good:
And, spite of pride in erring reason's spite,
One truth is clear, whatever is, is right.

—ALEXANDER POPE.
"Epistle I." *An Essay on Man. Moral Essays and Satires.*

One adequate support
For the calamities of mortal life
Exists—one only; an assured belief
That the procession of our fate, howe'er
Sad or disturbed, is ordered by a Being
Of infinite benevolence and power;
Whose everlasting purposes embrace
All accidents, converting them to good.

—WILLIAM WORDSWORTH.
"Book Fourth. Despondency Corrected." *The Excursion.*

 We are slow to wake up to a sense of the divinity that hedges us about. The great office of science has been to show us this universe as much more wonderful and divine than we have been wont to believe; shot through and through with celestial laws and forces; matter, indeed, but matter informed with spirit and intelligence; the creative energy inherent and active in the ground underfoot not less than in the stars and nebulae overhead.

—JOHN BURROUGHS.
"The Phantoms Behind Us." *Time and Change.*

We perceive everywhere proofs of Intelligence in the world of matter, - a something that knows and wills. It is not brute force, acting without knowledge and will, but an intelligent power, working by means well understood, continually directed to certain ends, which were meant to take place.

This intelligence let us call by the name of Mind, a power which knows without process of thought, wills without hesitation and choice; not mind with human limitations, but absolute.

The more comprehensively things are studied on a great scale, the more vast this mind appears in its far-reaching scope of time and space. The more minutely things are inquired after on a small scale, the more delicate appears this mind in its action. The solar system is not too big for it to grasp and hold, nor the eye of an aphis too small for it to finish off and provide for.

—THEODORE PARKER.
"Mind in the World of Matter." *The Collected Works of Theodore Parker: Vol. XIV.*

Before beginning, and without an end,
 As space eternal and as surety sure,
Is fixed a Power divine which moves to good,
 Only its laws endure.

This is its work upon the things ye see,
 The unseen things are more; men's hearts and minds,
The thoughts of peoples and their ways and wills,
 Those, too, the great Law binds.

Unseen it helpeth ye with faithful hands,
 Unheard it speaketh stronger than the storm.
Pity and Love are man's because long stress
 Moulded blind mass to form.

It will not be contemned of any one;
 Who thwarts it loses, and who serves it gains;
The hidden good it pays with peace and bliss,
 The hidden ill with pains.

It seeth everywhere and marketh all
 Do right—it recompenseth! do one wrong—
The equal retribution must be made,
 Though DHARMA tarry long.

—EDWIN ARNOLD.
The Light of Asia: Or, The Great Renunciation.

I dreamed a dream last night, when all was still,
When earth in sleep forgot her murmurings;
I saw the soul, the spirit—what you will—
Of this vast world; I saw the heart of things.

We call it real, this world of shapes and sounds,
These objects we can see and touch and hear,
Nor know we of the wonder-world that bounds
And thrills beneath, behind, the human ear.

I saw that back of everything there lies
This wondrous, shining essence, finer far
Than all the gathered gold of western skies
More lasting still than suns or planets are.

This, this is real, for this it is that gives
Life, color, motion, form, to what we see.
This hidden something that forever lives,
Sustaining all with subtle certainty.

In vain do men of science seek to prove
The hidden world that throbs behind the seen;
The ever-present Cause of things that move,
Eludes their searching sight, however keen.

As well might sunbeams seek to prove the sun
And rivulets the ocean, as that man—
A living flame from out the Central One—
Should seek to prove the Source where life began.

Within that unseen realm, all thought is born;
Each inspiration and each lofty theme
Is mothered there, and like a ray of morn
Comes shining down into the poet's dream.

We have an outlook on this world of forms,
While deeply rooted in the hidden sphere;
Impregnable to terrors and to storms,
The self-invisible knows naught of fear.

Would man but grasp, with focused powers of mind
The subtle laws that rule the finer realm,
Abandoning the lesser aims that blind,
The grosser joys that dull and overwhelm,

This dawning century would bring to light
The deepest truths for which we vainly grope;
Would open up new worlds to human sight,
In large fulfilment of our highest hope!

—A<small>NGELA</small> M<small>ORGAN</small>.
"Reality." Utterance And Other Poems.

For, from the first faint morn
Of life, the thirst for bliss
Deep in man's heart is born;
And, sceptic as he is,
He fails not to judge clear if this be quench'd or no.

Nor is the thirst to blame.
Man errs not that he deems
His welfare his true aim,
He errs because he dreams
The world does but exist that welfare to bestow.

We mortals are no kings
For each of whom to sway
A new-made world up-springs,
Meant merely for his play;
No, we are strangers here; the world is from of old.

In vain our pent wills fret,
And would the world subdue.

Limits we did not set
Condition all we do;
Born into life we are, and life must be our mould.

—MATTHEW ARNOLD.
"Empedocles on Etna." *Empedocles on Etna,*
and Other Poems.

The verdure sleeps in winter,
Awakes with April rain,
The sun swings low—'tis night,—ascends,
And lo! 'tis morn again:
The world spins on triumphant
Across a trackless sky,
And man seeks evermore in vain
The primal reason why.

O wither are we rushing?
And wherefrom were we torn?
We breathe from out the silences,
And breathless, back are borne.

Deep in the soul are voices
Returning this reply:
It took a God to make us,
Only God can answer why!

—GEORGIA DOUGLAS JOHNSON.
"Why." *Bronze: A Book of Verse.*

Through the changeful phases of life we are the executors of a will that is greater than our will, and that by this very fact sustains us. Give yourselves, with a good heart, to its service, and let it work through you.

—CHARLES WAGNER.
The Better Way.

Chapter 10

On Change, Rhythms, Ebb and Flow, Cycles

Turn, turn, my wheel! All things must change
To something new, to something strange;
Nothing that is can pause or stay;
The moon will wax, the moon will wane,
The mist and cloud will turn to rain,
The rain to mist and cloud again,
To-morrow be to-day.

Turn, turn, my wheel! All life is brief;
What now is bud will soon be leaf,
What now is leaf will soon decay;
The wind blows east, the wind blows west;
The blue eggs in the robin's nest
Will soon have wings and beak and breast,
And flutter and fly away.

—Henry Wadsworth Longfellow.
"Keramos." *Keramos and Other Poems.*

So the year in spring's mild hours
Loads the air with scent of flowers;
Summer paints the golden grain;

Then, when autumn comes again,
Bright with fruit the orchards glow;
Winter brings the rain and snow.
Thus the seasons' fixed progression,
Tempered in a due succession,
Nourishes and brings to birth
All that lives and breathes on earth.
Then, soon run life's little day,
All it brought it takes away.
But One sits and guides the reins,
He who made and all sustains;
King and Lord and Fountain-head,
Judge most holy, Law most dread;
Now impels and now keeps back,
Holds each waverer in the track.
Else, were once the power withheld
That the circling spheres compelled
In their orbits to revolve,
This world's order would dissolve,
And th' harmonious whole would all
In one hideous ruin fall.
But through this connected frame
Runs one universal aim;
Towards the Good do all things tend,
Many paths, but one the end.
For naught lasts, unless it turns
Backward in its course, and yearns
To that Source to flow again
Whence its being first was ta'en.

—BOETHIUS.
"Book IV. Song VI." *The Consolation of Philosophy of Boethius.*

The true Past departs not, nothing that was worthy in the Past departs; no Truth of Goodness realised by man ever dies, or can die; but is all still here, and, recognised or not, lives and works through endless changes. If all things, to speak in the German dialect, are discerned by us, and exist for us, in an element of Time, and therefore of Mortality and Mutability; yet Time itself reposes on Eternity: the truly Great and Transcendental has its basis and substance in Eternity; stands revealed to us as Eternity in a vesture of Time. Thus in all Poetry, Worship, Art, Society, as one form passes into another, nothing is lost; it is but the superficial, as it were the body only, that grows obsolete and dies; under the mortal body lies a soul which is immortal; which anew incarnates itself in fairer revelation; and the Present is the living sum-total of the whole Past.

In Change, therefore, there is nothing terrible, nothing supernatural: on the contrary, it lies in the very essence of our lot and life in this world. Today is not yesterday: we ourselves change; how can our Works and Thoughts, if they are always to be the fittest, continue always the same? Change, indeed, is painful; yet ever needful; and if Memory have its force and worth, so also has Hope.

—Thomas Carlyle.
"Characteristics."

In the degree that we employ ourselves we acquire Power. As nature, ever shifting and transforming, is most beautiful and delicious when it is not strictly either spring, or summer, or autumn; morning, noon, or night; so all the potency we ever possess is referable to our moments of action, or when we are experiencing or effecting Changes; the period of transition is that in which Power is developed; to acquire and to wield it we must be for ever seeking to quit the state we are in, and rise into a higher one. Power, accordingly, which is only Life under another name, is resolvable, essentially, into progression. It never consists in the *having been*, but always in the *becoming*.

—Leo Hartley Grindon.
"Chapter XVIII. Life Realized by Activity.—Action the Law of Happiness." *Life: Its Nature, Varieties, and Phenomena.*

Times go by turns and chances change by course,
From foul to fair, from better hap to worse.

The sea of Fortune doth not ever flow,
She draws her favours to the lowest ebb;
Her tides hath equal times to come and go,
Her loom doth weave the fine and coarsest web;
No joy so great but runneth to an end,
No hap so hard but may in fine amend.
Not always fall of leaf nor ever spring,
No endless night yet not eternal day;
The saddest birds a season find to sing,
The roughest storm a calm may soon allay:
Thus with succeeding turns God tempereth all,
That man may hope to rise, yet fear to fall.

—Robert Southwell.
"Times go by Turns." *The Oxford Book of English Verse: 1250–1900.*

*Press on! if Fortune play thee false
To-day, to-morrow she'll be true;
Whom now she sinks she now exalts,
Taking old gifts and granting new.
The wisdom of the present hour
Makes up for follies past and gone—
To weakness strength succeeds, and power
From frailty springs—press on! press on!*

—P\ark Benjamin.
"Press On."

If life is not always poetical, it is at least metrical. Periodicity rules over the mental experience of man, according to the path of the orbit of his thoughts. Distances are not gauged, ellipses not measured, velocities not ascertained, times not known. Nevertheless, the recurrence is sure. What the mind suffered last week, or last year, it does not suffer now; but it will suffer again next week or next year. Happiness is not a matter of events; it depends upon the tides of the mind.

Sorrow for one cause was intolerable yesterday, and will be intolerable tomorrow; today it is easy to bear, but the cause has not passed. Even the burden of a spiritual distress unsolved is bound to leave the heart to a temporary peace; and remorse itself does not remain—it returns. Gaiety takes us by a dear surprise. If we had made a course of notes of its visits, we might have been on the watch, and would have had an expectation instead of a discovery.

And life looks impossible to the young unfortunate, unaware of the inevitable and unfailing refreshment. It would be for their peace to learn that there is a tide in the affairs of men, in a sense more subtle—if it is not too audacious to add a meaning to Shakespeare—than the phrase was meant to contain. Their joy is flying away from them on its way home; their life will wax and wane; and if they would be wise, they must wake and rest in its phases, knowing that they are ruled by the law that commands all things.

—Alice Meynell.
"The Rhythm of Life." *The Rhythm of Life And Other Essays.*

Chapter 11

On Impermanence, Mortality, the March of Time

When we contemplate the close of life, the termination of man's designs and hopes; the silence that now reigns among those who, a little while ago, were so busy or so gay; who can avoid being touched with sensations at once awful and tender? What heart but then warms with the glow of humanity? In whose eye does not the tear gather, on revolving the fate of passing short lived man?"

"O vain and inconstant world! O fleeting and transient life. When will the sons of men learn to think of thee as they ought? When will they learn humanity from the affliction of their brethren; or moderation and wisdom, from a sense of their own fugitive state?"

—Ann Plato.
"Reflections on the close of life." *Essays: Including Biographies and Miscellaneous Pieces in Prose and Poetry.*

THERE was a time when meadow, grove, and stream,
  The earth, and every common sight,
    To me did seem
  Apparell'd in celestial light,

The glory and the freshness of a dream.
It is not now as it hath been of yore;—
  Turn wheresoe'er I may,
    By night or day,
The things which I have seen I now can see no more.

The rainbow comes and goes,
    And lovely is the rose;
    The moon doth with delight
  Look round her when the heavens are bare;
    Waters on a starry night
    Are beautiful and fair;
  The sunshine is a glorious birth;
  But yet I know, where'er I go,
That there hath pass'd away a glory from the earth.

What though the radiance which was once so bright
Be now for ever taken from my sight,
  Though nothing can bring back the hour
Of splendour in the grass, of glory in the flower;
    We will grieve not, rather find
    Strength in what remains behind;
    In the primal sympathy
    Which having been must ever be;
    In the soothing thoughts that spring
    Out of human suffering;
    In the faith that looks through death,
In years that bring the philosophic mind.

And O ye Fountains, Meadows, Hills, and Groves,
Forebode not any severing of our loves!
Yet in my heart of hearts I feel your might;
I only have relinquish'd one delight

To live beneath your more habitual sway.
I love the brooks which down their channels fret,
Even more than when I tripp'd lightly as they;
The innocent brightness of a new-born Day
    Is lovely yet;
The clouds that gather round the setting sun
Do take a sober colouring from an eye
That hath kept watch o'er man's mortality;
Another race hath been, and other palms are won.
Thanks to the human heart by which we live,
Thanks to its tenderness, its joys, and fears,
To me the meanest flower that blows can give
Thoughts that do often lie too deep for tears.

—WILLIAM WORDSWORTH.
Ode on Intimations of Immortality: From Recollections
of Early Childhood.

The Swan which boasted mid the tide,
Whose nest was guarded by the wave,
Floated for pleasure till she died,
And sunk beneath the flood to lave.

The bird of fashion drops her wing,
The rose-bush now declines to bloom;
The gentle breezes of the spring
No longer waft a sweet perfume.

Fair beauty with those lovely eyes,
Withers along her vital stream;
Proud fortune leaves her throne, and flies

From pleasure, as a flattering dream.

And gaudy mammon, sordid gain,
Whose plume has faded, once so gay,
Languishes mid her flowery train,
Whilst pleasure flies like fumes away.

Vain pleasures, O how short to last!
Like leaves which quick to ashes burn;
Which kindle from the slightest blast,
And slight to nothing hence return.

—GEORGE MOSES HORTON.
"The Swan - Vain Pleasures."

The secrets of the silence whence all come,
The secrets of the gloom whereto all go,
The life which lies between, like that arch flung
From cloud to cloud across the sky, which hath
Mists for its masonry and vapoury piers,
Melting to void again which was so fair
With sapphire hues, garnet, and chrysoprase.

—EDWIN ARNOLD.
The Light of Asia: Or, The Great Renunciation.

From low to high doth dissolution climb,
And sink from high to low, along a scale
Of awful notes, whose concord shall not fail;
A musical but melancholy chime,
Which they can hear who meddle not with crime,
Nor avarice, nor over-anxious care.

*Truth fails not; but her outward forms that bear
The longest date do melt like frosty rime,
That in the morning whitened hill and plain
And is no more; drop like the tower sublime
Of yesterday, which royally did wear
His crown of weeds, but could not even sustain
Some casual shout that broke the silent air,
Or the unimaginable touch of Time.*

—WILLIAM WORDSWORTH.
"Mutability." *Poems of Wordsworth.*

Chapter 12

ON UNITY, ONENESS

*You are plurality transformed into Unity,
And Unity passing into plurality;
This mystery is understood when man
Leaves the part and merges in the Whole.*

—MAHMUD SHABISTARI.
"Part IV. The Journey." *The Secret Rose Garden of Sa'd Ud Din Mahmud Shabistari.*

"Detached, separated! I say there is no such separation: nothing hitherto was ever stranded, cast aside; but all, were it only a withered leaf, works together with all; is borne forward on the bottomless, shoreless flood of Action, and lives through perpetual metamorphoses. The withered leaf is not dead and lost, there are Forces in it and around it, though working in inverse order; else how could it rot? Despise not the rag from which man makes Paper, or the litter from which the earth makes Corn. Rightly viewed no meanest object is insignificant; all objects are as windows, through which the philosophic eye looks into Infinitude itself."

—THOMAS CARLYLE.
"Book I. Chapter XI. Prospective." *Sartor Resartus.*

Turn, turn, my wheel! The human race,
Of every tongue, of every place,
Caucasian, Coptic, or Malay,
All that inhabit this great earth,
Whatever be their rank or worth,
Are kindred and allied by birth,
And made of the same clay.

—HENRY WADSWORTH LONGFELLOW.
"Keramos." *Keramos and Other Poems.*

There is one Great Law which exacts unconditional obedience, one unifying principle which is the basis of all diversity, one eternal Truth wherein all the problems of earth pass away like shadows. To realize this Law, this Unity, this Truth, is to enter into the Infinite, is to become one with the Eternal.

—JAMES ALLEN.
The Way of Peace.

There is one animal, one plant, one matter and one force. The laws of light and of heat translate each other;—so do the laws of sound and of colour; and so galvanism, electricity and magnetism are varied forms of the selfsame energy. While the student ponders this immense unity, he observes that all things in Nature, the animals, the mountain, the river, the seasons, wood, iron, stone, vapor, have a mysterious relation to his thoughts and his life; their growths, decays, quality and use so curiously resemble himself, in parts and in wholes, that he is compelled to speak by means of them. His words and his thoughts are framed by their help. Every noun is an

image. Nature gives him, sometimes in a flattered likeness, sometimes in caricature, a copy of every humor and shade in his character and mind. The world is an immense picture-book of every passage in human life. Every object he beholds is the mask of a man.
"The privates of man's heart
They speken and sound in his ear
As tho' they loud winds were;"
for the universe is full of their echoes.

—RALPH WALDO EMERSON.
"Poetry and Imagination." *Letters and Social Aims. Volume 8.*

All are but parts of one stupendous whole,
Whose body Nature is, and God the soul;
That, changed through all, and yet in all the same;
Great in the earth, as in the ethereal frame;
Warms in the sun, refreshes in the breeze,
Glows in the stars, and blossoms in the trees,
Lives through all life, extends through all extent,
Spreads undivided, operates unspent;
Breathes in our soul, informs our mortal part,
As full, as perfect, in a hair as heart:
As full, as perfect, in vile man that mourns,
As the rapt seraph that adores and burns:
To him no high, no low, no great, no small;
He fills, he bounds, connects, and equals all.

—ALEXANDER POPE.
"Epistle I." *An Essay on Man. Moral Essays and Satires.*

Do no violence to yourself, respect in yourself the oscillations of feeling. They are your life and your nature; One wiser than you ordained them. Do not abandon yourself altogether either to instinct or to will. Instinct is a siren, will a despot. Be neither the slave of your impulses and sensations of the moment, nor of an abstract and general plan; be open to what life brings from within and without, and welcome the unforeseen; but give to your life unity, and bring the unforeseen within the lines of your plan. Let what is natural in you raise itself to the level of the spiritual, and let the spiritual become once more natural. Thus will your development be harmonious, and the peace of heaven will shine upon your brow....

—HENRI-FRÉDÉRIC AMIEL.
Amiel's Journal. The Journal Intime of Henri-Frédéric Amiel.

Science tends more and more to reveal to us the unity that underlies the diversity of nature. We must have diversity in our practical lives; we must seize Nature by many handles. But our intellectual lives demand unity, demand simplicity amid all this complexity. Our religious lives demand the same. Amid all the diversity of creeds and sects we are coming more and more to see that religion is one, that verbal differences and ceremonies are unimportant, and that the fundamental agreements are alone significant.

—JOHN BURROUGHS.
"The Natural Providence." *Accepting the Universe. Essays in Naturalism.*

I can but lift the torch
Of Reason in the dusky cave of Life,
And gaze on this great miracle, the World,
Adoring That who made, and makes, and is,
And is not, what I gaze on—all else Form,
Ritual, varying with the tribes of men.

Well, I dream'd
That stone by stone I rear'd a sacred fane,
A temple, neither Pagod, Mosque, nor Church,
But loftier, simpler, always open-door'd
To every breath from heaven, and Truth and Peace
And Love and Justice came and dwelt therein.

—ALFRED LORD TENNYSON.
"Akbar's Dream." *The Death of Oenone, Akbar's Dream, and Other Poems.*

We of the twentieth century know better! We know that all religious aspiration, all sincere worship, can have but one source and one goal. We know that the God of the lettered and the unlettered, of the Greek and the barbarian, is after all the same God; and, like Peter, we perceive that He is no respecter of persons, but that in every nation he that feareth Him and worketh righteousness is acceptable to Him.

—CHARLES ALEXANDER EASTMAN (OHIYESA).
"Foreword." *The Soul of the Indian: An Interpretation.*

The masters of old attained unity with the Tao.
Heaven attained unity and became pure.

The earth attained unity and found peace.
The spirits attained unity so they could minister.
The valleys attained unity that they might be full.
Humanity attained unity that they might flourish.
Their leaders attained unity that they might set the example.
This is the power of unity.

—Lao-Tzu.
Tao Te Ching.

"Tis easy, as Experience may aver,
To pass from general to particular.
But most laborious to direct the soul
From studying parts, to reason on the whole:
Thoughts, train'd on narrow subjects, to let fall;
And learn the unison of each with all.

—Elizabeth Barrett Browning.
"An Essay on Mind." *An Essay on Mind, with Other Poems.*

The fact that there is a spiritual power in us, that is to say, a power which testifies to the unity of our life with the life of others, which impels us to regard others as other selves—this fact comes home to us even more forcibly in sorrow than in joy.

—Felix Adler.
Life and Destiny: Or, Thoughts from the Ethical Lectures of Felix Adler.

In the course of this progress each man learns by sad and bitter experience the intangible unity of all beings, finding that nothing that injures one can be good for any, that that which brings happiness to all can alone bring happiness to each. Not the happiness of the greater number but the happiness of all is necessary for the happiness of one.

Oneship is not in the lower but in the higher, not in the body or the mind but in the spirit, the divine, the eternal life. Virtue and happiness are ultimately the same, because virtue is that which serves the life of all, not the separated life, and it is virtue merely because it aids evolution and is lifting the many towards the One.

—Annie Besant.
"Problems of Ethics". *Some Problems of Life.*

How present and sensible to my inner sense is the unity of everything! It seems to me that I am able to pierce to the sublime motive which, in all the infinite spheres of existence, and through all the modes of space and time, every created form reproduces and sings within the bond of an eternal harmony.

—Henri-Frédéric Amiel.
Amiel's Journal. The Journal Intime of Henri-Frédéric Amiel.

Our language and many of our ideas and habits of thought date back to pre-scientific times—when there were two worlds, the heavenly and the earthly, separated by a gulf. Now we know that the two worlds are one, that they are inseparably blended; that the celestial and the terrestrial are under the same law; that we can never be any more in the heavens than we are here and now, nor any nearer the final sources of life and power; that the divine is underfoot as well as overhead; that we are part and parcel of the physical universe, and take our chances in the cosmic processes the same as the rest, and draw upon the same fund of animal life that the other creatures do. We are identified with the worm underfoot no less than with the stars overhead. We are not degraded by such a thought, but the whole of creation is lifted up. Our minds and bodies are not less divine, but all things are more divine. We have to gird up our loins and try to summon strength to see this tremendous universe as it is, alive and divine to the last particle and embosomed in the Infinite.

—JOHN BURROUGHS.
"The Phantoms Behind Us." *Time and Change.*

Things great and small,
We are but parts of the Eternal All;
We live not in a barren, baseless dream;
No endless, ineffectual chain
Of chance successions launched in vain;
But every beat of Time,
Each sun that shines or fails to shine,
Each animate life that comes to throb or cease,
Each life of herb or tree
Which springs aloft and then has ceased to be,
Each change of strife and peace,
Each soaring thought sublime,
Each deed of wrong and blood,

Each impulse towards an unattained good,—
All with a sure, unfaltering working tend
To one Ineffable, Beatific End.

—Lewis Morris.
"The Ode of Change." *The Ode of Life.*

There is a close analogy between the world of nature and the world of spirit. They bear the impress of the same hand; and hence the principles of nature and its laws are the types and shadows of the Invisible. Just as two books, though on different subjects, proceeding from the same pen, manifest indications of the thought of one mind, so the worlds, visible and invisible, are two books written by the same finger, and governed by the same idea. Or rather, they are but one book, separated into two only by the narrow range of our ken. For it is impossible to study the universe at all without perceiving that it is one system. Begin with what science you will, as soon as you get beyond the rudiments, you are constrained to associate it with another.

—Frederick William Robertson.
"Sermon 14. The Principle of Spiritual Harvest."
Sermons Preached at Brighton.

Chapter 13

On Cause and Effect, Conditionality, Interdependence

Being and non-being produce each other.
Difficult and easy complement each other.
Long and short define each other.
High and low oppose each other.
Fore and aft follow each other.

—Lao-Tzu
Tao Te Ching.

It seeth everywhere and marketh all
  Do right—it recompenseth! do one wrong—
The equal retribution must be made,
  Though DHARMA tarry long.

—Edwin Arnold.
The Light of Asia: Or, The Great Renunciation.

There is a process of seed-sowing in the mind and life a spiritual sowing which leads to a harvest according to the kind of seed sown. Thoughts, words, and acts are seeds sown, and, by the inviolable law of things, they produce after their kind.

He who would be blest, let him scatter blessings. He who would be happy, let him consider the happiness of others.

So in life, we get by giving; we grow rich by scattering.

—JAMES ALLEN.
Above Life's Turmoil.

What is their wisdom, clear and deep?—
That as men sow they surely reap,—
That every thought, that every deed,
Is sown into the soul for seed.

—EDWIN MARKHAM.
"One Life, One Law." *The Man with the Hoe And Other Poems.*

You reap what you sow - not something else, but that. An act of love makes the soul more loving. A deed of humbleness deepens humbleness. The thing reaped is the very thing sown, multiplied a hundred-fold. You have sown a seed of life; you reap life everlasting.

—FREDERICK WILLIAM ROBERTSON.
"Sermon 14. The Principle of Spiritual Harvest."
Sermons Preached at Brighton.

Every act rewards itself, or, in other words, integrates itself, in a twofold manner; first, in the thing, or in real nature; and secondly, in the circumstance, or in apparent nature. Men call the circumstance the retribution. The causal retribution is in the thing, and is seen by the soul. The retribution in the circumstance is seen by the understanding; it is inseparable from the thing, but is often spread over a long time, and so does not become distinct until after many years. The specific stripes may follow late after the offense, but they follow because they accompany it. Crime and punishment grow out of one stem. Punishment is a fruit that unsuspected ripens within the flower of the pleasure which concealed it. Cause and effect, means and ends, seed and fruit, cannot be severed; for the effect already blooms in the cause, the end preexists in the means, the fruit in the seed.

—RALPH WALDO EMERSON.
"Compensation." *Essays, First Series.*

That which ye sow ye reap. See yonder fields
  The sesamum was sesamum, the corn
Was corn. The Silence and the Darkness knew!
  So is a man's fate born.

He cometh, reaper of the things he sowed,
  Sesamum, corn, so much cast in past birth;
And so much weed and poison-stuff, which mar
  Him and the aching earth.

If he shall labour rightly, rooting these,
  And planting wholesome seedlings where they grew,
Fruitful and fair and clean the ground shall be,
  And rich the harvest due.

—EDWIN ARNOLD.
The Light of Asia: Or, The Great Renunciation.

…. that answer all must give
For all things done amiss or wrongfully,
Alone, each for himself, reckoning with that
The fixed arithmic of the universe,
Which meteth good for good and ill for ill,
Measure for measure, unto deeds, words, thoughts;
Watchful, aware, implacable, unmoved;
Making all futures fruits of all the pasts.

—Edwin Arnold.
The Light of Asia: Or, The Great Renunciation.

Chapter 14

On Reading, Books, Literature

I love my books as drunkards love their wine;
The more I drink, the more they seem divine;
With joy elate my soul in love runs o'er,
And each fresh draught is sweeter than before.
Books bring me friends where'er on earth I be,—
Solace of solitude,—bonds of society!
I love my books! they are companions dear,
Sterling in worth, in friendship most sincere;
Here talk I with the wise in ages gone,
And with the nobly gifted of our own.
If love, joy, laughter, sorrow please my mind,
Love, joy, grief, laughter in my books I find.

—Francis Bennoch.
"My Books." *The Storm, and Other Poems.*

If I were to pray for a taste which should stand me in stead under every variety of circumstances, and be a source of happiness and cheerfulness to me through life, and a shield against its ills, however things might go amiss, and the world frown upon me, it would be a taste for reading. I speak of it, of course, only as a worldly advantage, and not in the slightest degree as superseding or derogating from the higher office and surer and stronger panoply of religious principles, but as a taste, an instrument, and a mode of pleasurable gratification. Give a man this taste, and the means of gratifying it, and you can hardly fail of making a happy man, unless, indeed, you put into his hands a most perverse selection of books. You place him in contact with the best society in every period of history—with the wisest, the wittiest—with the tenderest, the bravest, and the purest characters that have adorned humanity. You make him a denizen of all nations—a contemporary of all ages. The world has been created for him.

—Sir John Herschel.
Address on the opening of the Eton Library, 1833.

I love vast libraries; yet there is a doubt
If one be better with them or without, -
Unless he use them wisely, and, indeed,
Knows the high art of what and how to read.
At Learning's fountain it is sweet to drink,
But 't is a nobler privilege to think;
And oft, from books apart, the thirsting mind
May make the nectar which it cannot find.
'T is well to borrow from the good and great;
'T is wise to learn; 't is godlike to create!

—John Godfrey Saxe.
"The Library." *The Poems of John Godfrey Saxe.*

The love of books is a love which requires neither justification, apology, nor defence. It is a good thing in itself: a possession to be thankful for, to rejoice over, to be proud of, and to sing praises for. With this love in his heart no man is ever poor, ever without friends, or the means of making his life lovely, beautiful, or happy. In prosperity or adversity, in joy or sorrow, in health or sickness, in solitude or crowded towns, books are never out of place, never without the power to comfort, console, and bless. They add wealth to prosperity, and make sweeter the sweet uses of adversity; they intensify joy and take the sting from, or give a bright relief to sorrow; they are the glorifiers of health and the blessed consolers of sickness; they people solitudes with the creations of thought, the children of fancy, and the offsprings of imagination, and to the busy haunts of men they lend a purpose and an aim, and tend to keep the heart unspotted in the world.

—JOHN ALFRED LANGFORD.
"Preliminary Essay." *The Praise of Books, As Said and Sung by English Authors.*

Speak low—tread softly through these halls;
Here genius lives enshrined,—
Here reign, in silent majesty,
The monarchs of the mind.
A mighty spirit-host they come,
From every age and clime;
Above the buried wrecks of years,
They breast the tide of Time.
And in their presence-chamber here,
They hold their regal state,
And round them throng a noble train,

The gifted and the great.
Oh, child of Earth! when round thy path
The storms of life arise,
And when thy brothers pass thee by,
With stern, unloving eyes,—
Here shall the Poets chant for thee
Their sweetest, loftiest lays;
And Prophets wait to guide thy steps
In wisdom's pleasant ways.
Come, with these God-anointed kings,
Be thou companion here;
And in thy mighty realm of mind,
Thou shalt go forth a peer!

—Anne C. Lynch.
"Thoughts in a Library."

Certainly the Art of Writing is the most miraculous of all things man has devised.

In Books lies the soul of the whole Past Time; the articulate audible voice of the Past, when the body and material substance of it has altogether vanished like a dream...

All that Mankind has done, thought, gained, or been; it is lying as in magic preservation in the pages of Books. They are the chosen possession of men.

—Thomas Carlyle.
"Lecture V. The Hero as Man of Letters." *On Heroes, Hero-worship and the Heroic in History.*

There is no Frigate like a Book
To take us Lands away,
Nor any Coursers like a Page
Of prancing Poetry.
This Traverse may the poorest take
Without oppress of Toll;
How frugal is the Chariot
That bears the Human Soul!

—Emily Dickinson.
"The Book." *Poems by Emily Dickinson. 3d series.*

Or else I sate on in my chamber green,
And lived my life, and thought my thoughts, and prayed
My prayers without the vicar; read my books,
Without considering whether they were fit
To do me good. Mark, there. We get no good
By being ungenerous, even to a book,
And calculating profits ... so much help
By so much reading. It is rather when
We gloriously forget ourselves, and plunge
Soul-forward, headlong, into a book's profound,
Impassioned for its beauty and salt of truth—
'Tis then we get the right good from a book.

—Elizabeth Barrett Browning.
Aurora Leigh.

An ordinary book needs but a subject: but a noble work must contain a germ which develops itself in the mind, like a plant There are no great compositions which have not been, at least, long pondered over, if not long worked at.

—Joseph Joubert.
"Of the Qualities of Authors." *Pensées of Joubert.*

On all sides, are we not driven to the conclusion that, of the things which man can do or make here below, by far the most momentous, wonderful and worthy are the things we call Books! Those poor bits of rag-paper with black ink on them;—from the Daily Newspaper to the sacred Hebrew Book, what have they not done, what are they not doing!— For indeed, whatever be the outward form of the thing (bits of paper, as we say, and black ink), is it not verily, at bottom, the highest act of man's faculty that produces a Book? It is the Thought of man; the true thaumaturgic virtue; by which man works all things whatsoever. All that he does, and brings to pass, is the vesture of a Thought.

—Thomas Carlyle.
"Lecture V. The Hero as Man of Letters." *On Heroes, Hero-worship and the Heroic in History.*

We moderns do not value our books as the ancients valued theirs, nor do we read them with their sincerity and reflection. They did not read for recreation merely, but for instruction. It was a serious business, to which they gave their minds as completely as the writers themselves had given their minds; for they felt, like Carlyle, that of all "things which man can do or make here below, by far the most momentous, wonderful, and worthy are the things we call books". The writers of antiquity were unceasing in their praise of books. They believed, with Cicero, that they are the food of youth; the delight of old age; the ornament of prosperity; the refuge and comfort of adversity...........

—Richard Henry Stoddard.
"Introduction." *The Golden Treasury of Poetry and Prose.*

It is fitting that we should pierce into the origins of human nature. It is right, too, that the great poets, the ideal interpreters of life, should be dearer to us than those who stop short with mere deciphering of what is real and actual. The poet has his own sphere of the beautiful and the sublime. But it is no less true that the enduring weight of historian, moralist, political orator, or preacher, depends on the amount of the wisdom of life that is hived in his pages. They may be admirable by virtue of other qualities, by learning, by grasp, by majesty of flight; but it is his moral sentences on mankind or the State, that rank the prose writer among the sages. These show that he has an eye for the great truths of action, for the permanent bearings of conduct, and for things that are for the guidance of all generations.

—John Morley.
Aphorisms—an address delivered before the Edinburgh Philosophical Institution, November 11, 1887.

For whatsoever things were written aforetime were written for our learning, that we through patience and comfort of the scriptures might have hope.

—Romans 15:4. *KJV.*

I fear we do not know what a power of immediate pleasure and permanent profit is to be had in a good book. The books which help you most are those which make you think the most.

But a great book that comes from a great thinker, - it is a ship of thought, deep freighted with truth, with beauty too. It sails the ocean, driven by the winds of heaven, breaking the level sea of life into beauty where it goes, leaving behind it a train of sparkling loveliness, widening as the ship goes on. And what treasures it brings to every land, scattering the seeds of truth, justice, love, and piety, to bless the world in ages yet to come.

—Theodore Parker.
"Books." *The Collected Works of Theodore Parker: Vol. XIV.*

Chapter 15

On Poetry and Poets

The Poet's License!—'t is the right,
Within the rule of duty,
To look on all delightful things
Throughout the world of beauty.

To gaze with rapture at the stars
That in the skies are glowing;
To see the gems of perfect dye
That in the woods are growing,
And more than sage astronomer,
And more than learned florist,
To read the glorious homilies
Of Firmament and Forest.

When Nature gives a gorgeous rose,
Or yields the simplest fern,
She writes this motto on the leaves,—
"To whom it may concern!"
And so it is the poet comes
And revels in her bowers.
And, though another hold the land,
Is owner of the flowers.

O, nevermore let Ignorance
With heedless iteration

> *Repeat the phrase as meaning aught*
> *Of trivial estimation;*
> *The Poet's License!—'t is the fee*
> *Of earth and sky and river*
> *To him who views them royally,*
> *To have and hold forever.*
>
> —JOHN GODFREY SAXE.
> "The Poet's License." *The Poems of John Godfrey Saxe.*

Poets take you about a wide and lovely world, they introduce you to hosts of delightful people, they make you love the common life and things near you, they set before you splendid heights of character which you admire and wish to climb. About all this they are never indifferent, but state all as having real values—love of good and fear of evil. Particularly they arouse genuine feeling in you about the rare new things you have never seen. Hence they fill you with expectation and make you wish to know more and more of life. But, just as much, they make you sensitive to the beauty and good of things familiar.

The great poets give you things to love, they make you believe in goodness and they portray our old earth as a brave good place to live and work in. In their pages, in spite of all that seems evil and all that is so, good men triumph at last, for

> "God's in his heaven,
> All's right with the world."
> —Browning: *Pippa Passes.*

The solutions they offer you are not worldly pay or success, not freedom from pain or work, but beauty—like the dawn of a sweet May morning: and peace—like waters on starry nights: and companionship—like a good friend for a walk in the woods: and the love of God—that "friend that sticketh closer than a brother": and the sense of a never-ending life.

—WILLIAM DARNALL MACCLINTOCK.
"Introductory Essay. Young People and the Poets."
The World's Best Poetry.

Poetry is itself a thing of God;
He made His prophets poets: and the more
We feel of poesie do we become
Like God in love and power,—under-makers.
And song is of the supernatural
Natural utterance; and solely can
Speak the unbounded beauty of the world,
And the premortal concords of pure mind.
All great lays, equals to the minds of men,
Deal more or less with the Divine, and have
For end some good of mind or soul of man.

—PHILIP JAMES BAILEY.
"Proem." *Festus: A Poem.*

Poet. Go to, and find thyself another slave!
What! and the lofty birthright Nature gave,
The noblest talent Heaven to man has lent,
Thou bid'st the Poet fling to folly's ocean!
How does he stir each deep emotion?

How does he conquer every element?
But by the tide of song that from his bosom springs,
And draws into his heart all living things?
When Nature's hand, in endless iteration,
The thread across the whizzing spindle flings,
When the complex, monotonous creation
Jangles with all its million strings:
Who, then, the long, dull series animating,
Breaks into rhythmic march the soulless round?
And, to the law of All each member consecrating,
Bids one majestic harmony resound?
Who bids the tempest rage with passion's power?
The earnest soul with evening-redness glow?
Who scatters vernal bud and summer flower
Along the path where loved ones go?
Who weaves each green leaf in the wind that trembles
To form the wreath that merit's brow shall crown?
Who makes Olympus fast? the gods assembles?
The power of manhood in the Poet shown.

—JOHANN WOLFGANG VON GOETHE.
"Prelude in the Theatre." *Faust: A Tragedy,* translated from the German of Goethe.

In poetry we say we require the miracle. The bee flies among the flowers, and gets mint and marjoram, and generates a new product, which is not mint and marjoram, but honey; the chemist mixes hydrogen and oxygen to yield a new product, which is not these, but water; and the poet listens to conversation and beholds all objects in Nature, to give back, not them, but a new and transcendent whole.

Poetry is the perpetual endeavor to express the spirit of the thing, to pass the brute body and search the life and reason which causes it to exist;—to see that the object is always flowing away, whilst the spirit or necessity which causes it subsists. Its essential mark is that it betrays in every word instant activity of mind, shown in new uses of every fact and image, in preternatural quickness or perception of relations. All its words are poems. It is a presence of mind that gives a miraculous command of all means of uttering the thought and feeling of the moment. The poet squanders on the hour an amount of life that would more than furnish the seventy years of the man that stands next him.

—Ralph Waldo Emerson.
"Poetry and Imagination." *Letters and Social Aims.*
Volume 8.

His home is on the heights: to him
Men wage a battle weird and dim,
Life is a mission stern as fate,
And Song a dread apostolate.
The toils of prophecy are his,
To hail the coming centuries—
To ease the steps and lift the load
Of souls that falter on the road.
The perilous music that he hears
Falls from the vortices of the spheres.

He presses on before the race,
And sings out of a silent place.
Like faint notes of a forest bird
On heights afar that voice is heard;

And the dim path he trods today
Will sometime be a trodden way.
But when the race comes toiling on
That voice of wonder will be gone—
Be heard on higher peaks afar,
Moved upward with the morning star.

O men of earth, that wandering voice
Still goes the upward way: Rejoice!

—Edwin Markham.
"The Poet." *The Man with the Hoe, and Other Poems.*

Of poetry in general, however, I will say: I am not of those "who think a poet and a bell-ringer to be equals." I do not believe poetry is on the decline. I do not believe that human advancement extinguishes the torch of sentiment. I cannot think that money getting is the whole business of man. Rather am I convinced that the world is approaching a poetical revolution. The subtle evolutions of thought must yet be expressed in song. "Poesy," says one, "is the language of the imagination." Campbell said, "it is the eloquence of truth." As we understand it to-day, I think poetry is the language of universal sentiment. Torch of the unresting mind, she kindles in advance of all progress. Her waitings are on the threshold of the infinite where, beckoning man to listen, she interprets the leaves of immortality. Her voice is the voice of Eternity dwelling in all great souls. Her aims are the inducements of heaven, and her triumphs, the survival of the Beautiful, the True, and the Good. In her language there is no mistaking of that liberal thought which is the health of mind. A secret interpreter, she waits not for data, phenomena, and manifestations, but anticipates and spells the wishes of Heaven.

Poesy is fair, and to her all things are fair: the rain prophesies, and seasons and soil give testimony that God is a friend of all His creatures, and man is His delight. In great forests she sees temples reared and hears the sounds of praise. The dumb rocks are silent, but express all real prayer.

Poesy is free, and knows not of hire. Beauty is her inspiration,—her creed is Truth, and Goodness her Divinity. The first she praises, magnifies the second, and adores the third. And to end all, in her divine right a teacher, she brings benefits even to the lowly.

—ALBERY ALLSON WHITMAN.
"Dedicatory Address." *The Rape of Florida.*

The poet hath a realm within, and throne,
And in his own soul, singeth his lament.
A comer often in the world unknown—
A flaming minister to mortals sent;
In an apocalypse of sentiment,
He shows in colors true the right or wrong,
And lights the soul of virtue with content;
Oh! could the world without him please us long!
What truth is there that lives and does not live in song?

—ALBERY ALLSON WHITMAN.
"Canto 1. Invocation." *The Rape of Florida.*

Poetry is the record of the best and happiest moments of the happiest and best minds. We are aware of evanescent visitations of thought and feeling sometimes associated with place or person, sometimes regarding our own mind alone, and always arising unforeseen and departing unbidden, but elevating and delightful beyond all expression; so that even in the desire and regret they leave, there cannot but be pleasure, participating as it does in the nature of its object.

Poetry thus makes immortal all that is best and most beautiful in the world; it arrests the vanishing apparitions which haunt the interlunations of life, and veiling them, or in language or in form, sends them forth among mankind, bearing sweet news of kindred joy to those with whom their sisters abide—abide, because there is no portal of expression from the caverns of the spirit which they inhabit into the universe of things. Poetry redeems from decay the visitations of the divinity in man.

Poetry turns all things to loveliness; it exalts the beauty of that which is most beautiful, and it adds beauty to that which is most deformed; it marries exultation and horror, grief and pleasure, eternity and change; it subdues to union under its light yoke, all irreconcilable things. It transmutes all that it touches, and every form moving within the radiance of its presence is changed by wondrous sympathy to an incarnation of the spirit which it breathes: its secret alchemy turns to potable gold the poisonous waters which flow from death through life; it strips the veil of familiarity from the world, and lays bare the naked and sleeping beauty, which is the spirit of its forms.

—Percy Bysshe Shelley.
"A Defence of Poetry." *A Defence of Poetry and Other Essays.*

The poetry of mysticism might be defined on the one hand as a temperamental reaction to the vision of Reality: on the other, as a form of prophecy. As it is the special vocation of the mystical consciousness to mediate between two orders, going out in loving adoration towards God and coming home to tell the secrets of Eternity to other men; so the artistic self-expression of this consciousness has also a double character. It is love-poetry, but love-poetry which is often written with a missionary intention. Kabîr's songs are of this kind: out-births at once of rapture and of charity.

—Evelyn Underhill
"Introduction." *Songs of Kabir*. Translated by Rabindranath Tagore.

The springs of the truest prayer and of the deepest poetry—twin expressions of man's outward-going passion for that Eternity which is his home—rise very near together in the heart.

—Evelyn Underhill.
"The Place of Will, Intellect, and Feeling in Prayer."
The Essentials of Mysticism and Other Essays.

We shall reach, however, more immediately a distinct conception of what the true Poetry is, by mere reference to a few of the simple elements which induce in the Poet himself the poetical effect. He recognizes the ambrosia which nourishes his soul in the bright orbs that shine in Heaven—in the volutes of the flower—in the clustering of low shrubberies—in the waving of the grain-fields—in the slanting of tall eastern trees—in the blue distance of mountains—in the grouping of clouds—in the twinkling of half-hidden brooks—in the gleaming of silver rivers—in the repose of sequestered lakes—in the star-mirroring depths of lonely wells. He perceives it in the songs of birds—in the harp of Bolos—in the sighing of the night-wind—in the repining voice of the forest—in the surf that complains to the shore—in the fresh breath of the woods—in the scent of the violet—in the voluptuous perfume of the hyacinth—in the suggestive odour that comes to him at eventide from far distant undiscovered islands, over dim oceans, illimitable and unexplored. He owns it in all noble thoughts—in all unworldly motives—in all holy impulses—in all chivalrous, generous, and self-sacrificing deeds.

—EDGAR ALLAN POE.
"The Poetic Principle." *The Complete Poetical Works of Edgar Allan Poe.*

No doubt a man may be truly, deeply religious who has little or no development on the æsthetic side, to whom poetry makes no special appeal. But it is certain that he whose soul is deaf to the "concord of sweet sounds" misses a mighty aid in the spiritual life. For a hymn is a wing by which the spirit soars above earthly cares and trials into a purer air and a clearer sunshine. Nothing can better scatter the devils of melancholy and gloom or doubt and fear. When praise and prayer, trust and love, faith and hope, and similar sentiments, have passed into and through some poet's passionate soul, until he has become so charged with them that he has been able to fix them in a form of expression where beauty is united to strength, where concentration and ornamentation are alike secured, then the deepest needs of great numbers are fully met. What was vague and dim is brought into light. What was only half conceived, and so but half felt, is made to grip the soul with power. Poetry is of the very highest value for the inspiration and guidance of life, for calling out the emotions and opening up spiritual visions. It carries truths not only into the understanding, but into the heart, where they are likely to have the most direct effect on conduct.

—JAMES MUDGE.
"Preface." *Poems with Power to Strengthen the Soul.*

There is in all great poets a wisdom of humanity which is superior to any talents they exercise. The author, the wit, the partisan, the fine gentleman, does not take place of the man. Humanity shines in Homer, in Chaucer, in Spenser, in Shakespeare, in Milton. They are content with truth.

—RALPH WALDO EMERSON.
"The Over-Soul." *Essays, First Series.*

For Poesy's whole essence, when defined,
Is elevation of the reasoning mind,
When inward sense from Fancy's page is taught,
And moral feeling ministers to Thought.
And hence, the natural passions all agree
In seeking Nature's language—poetry.

—ELIZABETH BARRETT BROWNING.
"An Essay on Mind." *An Essay on Mind, with Other Poems.*

It is almost impossible to take too extended a view of the nature and character of Poetry. All the strange vicissitudes of human life,—all the harmonious beauty of the Universe,—all the incomprehensible sublimity of the Supreme Being is Poetry, in the widest and most significant sense of the word. Whatever excites our wonder and imagination, awakens our best sympathies, and stirs up the hidden depths of our passions, is Poetry; inasmuch as it brings into exercise the moral and intellectual faculties of the mind.

—John Critchley Prince.
"Random Thoughts on Poetry." *Hours with the Muses.*

Chapter 16

ON WORK, LABOR, TOIL

Work thou for pleasure; paint or sing or carve
The thing thou lovest, though the body starve.
Who works for glory misses oft the goal;
Who works for money coins his very soul;
Work for the work's sake, then, and it may be
That these things shall be added unto thee.

—Kenyon Cox.
"The Gospel of Art." *Hoyt's New Cyclopedia*
of Practical Quotations.

'Religion,' I said; for properly speaking, all true Work is Religion: and whatsoever Religion is not Work may go and dwell among the Brahmins, Antinomians, Spinning Dervishes, or where it will; with me it shall have no harbour. Admirable was that of the old Monks, _'Laborare est Orare, Work is Worship.'

Older than all preached Gospels was this unpreached, inarticulate, but ineradicable, forever-enduring Gospel: Work, and therein have well-being.

—Thomas Carlyle.
"Chapter 12. Reward." *Past and Present.*

Who only asks for humblest wealth,
Enough for competence and health;
And leisure, when his work is done,
To read his book by chimney-nook,
Or stroll at setting of the sun.
Who toils, as every man should toil,
For fair reward, erect and free:
These are the men - the best of men -
These are the men we mean to be!

—Charles Mackay.
"Daily Work." *Voices from the Mountains and from the Crowd.*

The true husbandman will cease from anxiety, as the squirrels manifest no concern whether the woods will bear chestnuts this year or not, and finish his labor with every day, relinquishing all claim to the produce of his fields, and sacrificing in his mind not only his first but his last fruits also.

—Henry David Thoreau
"The Bean-Field." *Walden.*

Be sure, no earnest work
Of any honest creature, howbeit weak,
Imperfect, ill-adapted, fails so much,
It is not gathered as a grain of sand
To enlarge the sum of human action used
For carrying out God's end. No creature works
So ill, observe, that therefore he's cashiered.

The honest earnest man must stand and work;
The woman also......

> —Elizabeth Barrett Browning.
> *Aurora Leigh.*

Labour is rest—from the sorrows that greet us;
Rest from all petty vexations that meet us,
Rest from sin-promptings that ever entreat us,
Rest from world-syrens that lure us to ill.
Work—and pure slumbers shall wait on thy pillow;
Work—thou shalt ride over Care's coming billow;
Lie not down wearied 'neath Woe's weeping-willow!
Work with a stout heart and resolute will!

Droop not, tho' shame, sin, and anguish are round thee!
Bravely fling off the cold chain that hath bound thee!
Look to yon pure Heaven smiling beyond thee!
Rest not content in thy darkness—a clod!
Work—for some good,—be it ever so slowly!
Cherish some flower,—be it ever so lowly!
Labour! all labour is noble and holy!—
Let thy great deeds be thy prayer to thy God!

> —Frances Sargent Osgood.
> "Labour." *The Poets and Poetry of America:*
> *With an Historical Introduction.*

Leave this chanting and singing and telling of beads!
Whom dost thou worship in this lonely dark corner of a
temple with doors all shut? Open thine eyes and see thy

God is not before thee!
He is there where the tiller is tilling the hard ground and where the pathmaker is breaking stones. He is with them in sun and in shower, and his garment is covered with dust. Put off thy holy mantle and even like him come down on the dusty soil!
Deliverance? Where is this deliverance to be found? Our master himself has joyfully taken upon him the bonds of creation; he is bound with us all for ever.
Come out of thy meditations and leave aside thy flowers and incense! What harm is there if thy clothes become tattered and stained? Meet him and stand by him in toil and in sweat of thy brow.

—RABINDRANATH TAGORE.
Gitanjali (Song Offerings).

If we would be really wise, we must diligently apply ourselves, and confront the same continuous application which our forefathers did; for labour is still, and ever will be, the inevitable price set upon everything which is valuable. We must be satisfied to work with a purpose, and wait the results with patience. All progress, of the best kind, is slow; but to him who works faithfully and zealously the reward will, doubtless, be vouchsafed in good time.

—SAMUEL SMILES.
Self-help; with illustrations of character and conduct.

In work, then, consists the true pride of life; grounded in active employment, though early ardor may abate, it never degenerates into indifference, and age, as we have said before, lives in perennial youth. Life is a weariness only to the idle, or where the soul is empty.

—Leo Hartley Grindon.
"Chapter XVIII. Life Realized by Activity.—Action the Law of Happiness." *Life: Its Nature, Varieties, and Phenomena.*

It is a very busy world in which we mortals meet,
There are so many weary hands, so many tired feet;
So many, many tasks are born with every morning's sun.
And though we labor with a will the work seems never done.
And yet for every moment's task there comes a moment's time:
The burden and the strength to bear are like a perfect rhyme.
The heart makes strong the honest hand, the will seeks out the way,
Nor must we do to-morrow's work, nor yesterday's, to-day.
We scale the mountain's rugged side, not at one mighty leap,
But step by step and breath by breath we climb the lofty steep.
Each simple duty comes alone our willing strength to try;
One little moment at a time and so the days go by.
With strength to lift and heart to hope, we strive from sun to sun,
A little here, a little there, and all our tasks are done;
There's time to toil and time to sing and time for us to play,
Nor must we do to-morrow's work, nor yesterday's, to-day.

—Nixon Waterman.
"This Busy World." *The Girl Wanted.*

'Tis much to know in life our proper task,
Yet more to do, when well we know our work;
Into Life's harvest none are sent to shirk—

Of others' toil the gifts of labor ask;

Only in doing may the arm grow strong,
The mind be strengthened in its own high thought:
And ours—ours only what our hands have wrought,
The sole sure wages that to Toil belong.
Do then thy task, and trust the gods' decree,
That as thy work thy recompense shall be.

—BENJAMIN HATHAWAY.
"Work." *Art-life And Other Poems.*

Life should be full of earnest work,
Our hearts undashed by fortune's frown;
Let perseverance conquer fate,
And merit seize the victor's crown.

—PHOEBE CARY.
"Aspirations."

Thus all must work—with head or hand,
For self or others, good or ill;
Life is ordained to bear, like land,
Some fruit, be fallow as it will:
Evil has force itself to sow
Where we deny the healthy seed,—
And all our choice is this,—to grow
Pasture and grain or noisome weed.

Then in content possess your hearts,
Unenvious of each other's lot,—
For those which seem the easiest parts

Have travail which ye reckon not:
And He is bravest, happiest, best,
Who, from the task within his span,
Earns for himself his evening rest
And an increase of good for man.

—RICHARD MONCKTON MILNES.
"Labour." *Poems of Many Years.* Edward Moxon, 1844.

Yet life is not a vision nor a prayer,
But stubborn work; she may not shun her task.
After the first compassion, none will spare
Her portion and her work achieved, to ask.
She pleads for respite,—she will come ere long
When, resting by the roadside, she is strong.

Nay, for the hurrying throng of passers-by
Will crush her with their onward-rolling stream.
Much must be done before the brief light die;
She may not loiter, rapt in the vain dream.
With unused trembling hands, and faltering feet,
She staggers forth, her lot assigned to meet.
But when she fills her days with duties done,
Strange vigor comes, she is restored to health.
New aims, new interests rise with each new sun,
And life still holds for her unbounded wealth.
All that seemed hard and toilsome now proves small,
And naught may daunt her,—she hath strength for all.

—EMMA LAZARUS.
"Work." *The Poems of Emma Lazarus. Narrative, Lyric,*
and Dramatic.

Chapter 17

On Time

Up, 'tis no dreaming-time! awake! awake!
For He who sits on the High Judge's seat
Doth in his record note each wasted hour,
Each idle word. Take heed thy shrinking soul
Find not their weight too heavy when it stands
At that dread bar from whence is no appeal.
For while we trifle the light sand steals on,
Leaving the hour-glass empty. So thy life
Glideth away. Stamp wisdom on its hours.

—Lydia Howard Sigourney.
"True Wisdom". *Pocahontas, and Other Poems.*

Now! it is gone.—Our brief hours travel post,
Each with its thought or deed, its Why or How:—
But know, each parting hour gives up a ghost
To dwell within thee-an eternal NOW!

—Samuel Taylor Coleridge.
"Inscription for a Time-Piece." *The Poems of Samuel Taylor Coleridge.*

"For what is Time? The shadow on the dial,—the striking of the clock,—the running of the sand,—day and night,—summer and winter,—months, years, centuries! These are but arbitrary and outward signs,—the measure of Time, not Time itself! Time is the Life of the Soul. If not this, then tell me what it is?"

—Henry Wadsworth Longfellow.
"Book II. Chapter VI. Glimpses into Cloud-land."
Hyperion: A Romance.

Time is the most undefinable yet paradoxical of things; the past is gone, the future is not come, and the present becomes the past, even while we attempt to define it, and like the flash of the lightning, at once exists and expires.—

Time is the measurer of all things, but is itself immeasurable, and the grand discloser of all things, but is itself undisclosed. Like space, it is incomprehensible, because it has no limit, and it would be still more so, if it had.

—Charles Caleb Colton.
"DLXXXVII." *Lacon: Or, Many Things in Few Words; Addressed to Those who Think.*

The dew even in the deepest and most tangled grass has long since been dried, and some of the flowers that close at noon will shortly fold their petals. The morning airs, which breathe so sweetly, come less and less frequently as the heat increases. Vanishing from the sky, the last fragments of cloud have left an untarnished azure. Many times the bees have returned to their hives, and thus the index of the day advances. It is nothing to the greenfinches; all their thoughts are in their song-talk. The sunny moment is to them all in all. So deeply are they rapt in it that they do not know whether it is a moment or a year. There is no clock for feeling, for joy, for love.

—Richard Jefferies.
The Pageant of Summer.

That great mystery of Time, were there no other; the illimitable, silent, never-resting thing called Time, rolling, rushing on, swift, silent, like an all-embracing ocean-tide, on which we and all the Universe swim like exhalations, like apparitions which are, and then are not: this is forever very literally a miracle; a thing to strike us dumb,—for we have no word to speak about it.

—Thomas Carlyle.
"Lecture 1. The Hero as Divinity." *On Heroes, Hero-worship and the Heroic in History.*

Listen to the water-mill,
Through the live-long day;
How the clicking of its wheel
Wears the hours away!
Languidly the autumn wind
Stirs the forest leaves,
From the fields the reapers sing,
Binding up the sheaves;
And a proverb haunts my mind
As a spell is cast,

"The mill cannot grind
With the water that is past."

Autumn winds revive no more
Leaves that once are shed,
And the sickle cannot reap
Corn once gathered;
Flows the ruffled streamlet on,
Tranquil, deep and still;
Never gliding back again
To the water-mill;
Truly speaks that proverb old
With a meaning vast—
" The mill cannot grind
With the water that has past."

Take the lesson to thyself,
True and loving heart;
Golden youth is fleeting by,
Summer hours depart;
Learn to make the most of life,
Lose no happy day!
Time will never bring thee back,
Chances swept away!
Leave no tender word unsaid,
Love while love shall last;
" The mill cannot grind
With the water that is past. "

—Sarah Doudney.
"The Lesson of the Water-Mill."

The every-day cares and duties which men call drudgery are the weights and counterpoises of the clock of time, giving its pendulum a true vibration, and its hands a regular motion; and when they cease to hang upon the wheels, the pendulum no longer sways, the hands no longer move, the clock stands still.

—Henry Wadsworth Longfellow.
Kavanagh, A Tale.

On many an idle day have I grieved over lost time. But it is never lost, my lord. Thou hast taken every moment of my life in thine own hands.
Hidden in the heart of things thou art nourishing seeds into sprouts, buds into blossoms, and ripening flowers into fruitfulness.
I was tired and sleeping on my idle bed and imagined all work had ceased. In the morning I woke up and found my garden full with wonders of flowers.

—Rabindranath Tagore.
Gitanjali (Song Offerings).

Time is endless in thy hands, my lord. There is none to count thy minutes.
Days and nights pass and ages bloom and fade like flowers. Thou knowest how to wait.
Thy centuries follow each other perfecting a small wild flower. We have no time to lose, and having no time we must scramble for our chances. We are too poor to be late.
And thus it is that time goes by while I give it to every

querulous man who claims it, and thine altar is empty of all offerings to the last.

At the end of the day I hasten in fear lest thy gate be shut; but I find that yet there is time.

—RABINDRANATH TAGORE.
Gitanjali (Song Offerings).

Meanwhile, we too admit that the present is an important time; as all present time necessarily is. The poorest Day that passes over us is the conflux of two Eternities; it is made up of currents that issue from the remotest Past, and flow onwards into the remotest Future. We were wise indeed, could we discern truly the signs of our own time; and by knowledge of its wants and advantages, wisely adjust our own position in it. Let us, instead of gazing idly into the obscure distance, look calmly around us, for a little, on the perplexed scene where we stand. Perhaps, on a more serious inspection, something of its perplexity will disappear, some of its distinctive characters and deeper tendencies more clearly reveal themselves; whereby our own relations to it, our own true aims and endeavours in it, may also become clearer.

—THOMAS CARLYLE.
"Signs of the Times."

After we come to mature years, there is nothing of which we are so vividly conscious as of the swiftness of time. Its brevity and littleness are the theme of poets, moralists, and preachers. Yet there is nothing of which there is so much—

nor day nor night, ocean nor sky, winter nor summer equal it. It is a perpetual flow from the inexhaustible fountains of eternity:—And we have no adequate conception of our earthly life until we think of it and live in it as a part of forever. *Now* is eternity......

—HORATIO STEBBINS.

'Tis a mistake: time flies not,
He only hovers on the wing:
Once born, the moment dies not,
'Tis an immortal thing;
While all change is beneath the sky,
Fix'd like the sun as learned sages prove,
Though from our moving world he seems to move,
'Tis time stands still, and we that fly.

There is no past; from nature's birth,
Days, months, years, ages, till the end
Of these revolving heavens and earth,
All to one centre tend;

—What has been is, what is shall last;
The present is the focus of the past;
The future, perishing as it arrives,
Becomes the present, and itself survives.

Time is not progress, but amount;
One vast accumulating store,
Laid up, not lost;—we do not count
Years gone but added to the score
Of wealth untold, to clime nor class confined,

Riches to generations lent,
For ever spending, never spent,
The august inheritance of all mankind.

Of this from Adam to his latest heir,
All in due turn their portion share,
Which, as they husband or abuse,
Their souls they win or lose.

—James Montgomery.
"Time: A Rhapsody." *A Poet's Portfolio; or, Minor Poems: in Three Books.*

Chapter 18

ON MUSIC, SONG, DANCE

*'Tis said, the pipe and lute that charm our ears
Derive their melody from rolling spheres;
But Faith, o'erpassing speculation's bound,
Can see what sweetens every jangled sound.
We, who are parts of Adam, heard with him
The song of angels and of seraphim.
Our memory, though dull and sad, retains
Some echo still of those unearthly strains.
Oh, music is the meat of all who love,
Music uplifts the soul to realms above.
The ashes glow, the latent fires increase:
We listen and are fed with joy and peace.*

—RUMI (JALĀL AD-DĪN MUHAMMAD RŪMĪ).
"Remembered Music."

Music is well said to be the speech of angels; in fact, nothing among the utterances allowed to man is felt to be so divine. It brings us near to the infinite; we look for moments, across the cloudy elements, into the eternal sea of light, when song leads and inspires us. Serious nations, all nations that can still listen to the mandate of nature, have prized song and music as the highest; as a vehicle for worship, for prophecy, and for whatsoever in them was divine. Their singer was a vates, admitted to the council of the universe, friend of the gods, and choicest benefactor to man.

—Thomas Carlyle.
"The Opera." *The Works of Thomas Carlyle: Critical and Miscellaneous Essays.*

The Father spake! In grand reverberations
Through space rolled on the mighty music-tide,
While to its low, majestic modulations,
The clouds of chaos slowly swept aside

Nor yet has ceased that sound—his love revealing
Though, in response, a universe moves by!
Throughout eternity, its echo pealing—
World after world awakes in glad reply!

And wheresoever, in his rich creation,
Sweet music breathes—in wave, or bird, or soul—
'Tis but the faint and far reverberation
Of that great tune to which the planets roll!

—Frances S. Osgood.
"Music." *The Female Poets of America.*

I have sometimes thought that only the elevated and elegant language of poetry should be employed in describing music: for music is poetry, and poetry is music; that is, in many of their characteristics they are one and the same. But, to put this idea in another form, let us say that Music is the beautiful sister of Poetry, that other soul-expressing medium; and

who would create the latter must commune with the former, and be able to bring to his uses the sweet and finishing graces of her rhythmic forms. In early times, the qualities of the poet and musician were generally actually united in the same person. The poet usually set to music, and in most instances sang, his effusions. Nor to this day have the
> "Poets, who on earth have made us heirs
> Of truth and pure delight by heavenly lays,"

ceased to sing, in bewitching verse, the noble qualities of music.

—James M. Trotter.
"A Description of Music." *Music and Some Highly Musical People.*

Music resembles poetry, in each
Are nameless graces which no methods teach,
And which a master-hand alone can reach.

—Alexander Pope.
An Essay on Criticism. Part 1.

A man should hear a little music, read a little poetry, and see a fine picture, every day of his life, in order that worldly cares may not obliterate the sense of the beautiful which God has implanted in the human soul.

—Johann Wolfgang von Goethe.
"#196." *Musical Mosaics: A Collection of Six Hundred Selections from Musical Literature, Ancient and Modern.*

Listen to the whisper of the wind blowing through the pine-trees or to the murmur of a stream running over the stones: we may observe that in them there is the music of nature. Gaze at the wreath of smoke creeping under the green grass or at the shadow of clouds reflected in the water: we know that the universe has its own masterpieces of literary composition.

—Hung Ying-Ming.
Musings of a Chinese Vegetarian.

My cot was down by a cypress grove,
And I sat by my window the whole night long,
And heard well up from the deep dark wood
A mocking-bird's passionate song.

And I thought of myself so sad and lone,
And my life's cold winter that knew no spring;
Of my mind so weary and sick and wild,
Of my heart too sad to sing.

But e'en as I listened the mock-bird's song,
A thought stole into my saddened heart,
And I said, "I can cheer some other soul
By a carol's simple art."

For oft from the darkness of hearts and lives
Come songs that brim with joy and light,
As out of the gloom of the cypress grove
The mocking-bird sings at night.

So I sang a lay for a brother's ear
In a strain to soothe his bleeding heart,
And he smiled at the sound of my voice and lyre,

Though mine was a feeble art.

But at his smile I smiled in turn,
And into my soul there came a ray:
In trying to soothe another's woes
Mine own had passed away.

—Paul Laurence Dunbar.
"The Lesson." *Lyrics of Lowly Life.*

The wave of the ocean, the leaf of the wood,
In the rhythm of motion proclaim life is good.
The stars are all swinging to metres and rhyme,
The planets are singing while suns mark the time.
The moonbeams and rivers float off in a trance,
The Universe quivers—on, on with the dance!
Our partners we pick from the best of the throng
In the ballroom of Life and go lilting along;
We follow our fancy, and choose as we will,
For waltz or for tango or merry quadrille;
But ever one partner is waiting us all
At the end of the programme, to finish the ball.
Unasked, and unwelcome, he comes without leave
And calls when he chooses, 'My dance, I believe?'
And none may refuse him, and none may say no;
When he beckons the dancer, the dancer must go.
You may hate him, and shun him; and yet in life's ball
For the one who lives well 'tis the best dance of all.

—Ella Wheeler Wilcox.
"The Last Dance". *Poems of Optimism.*

A musical thought is one spoken by a mind that has penetrated into the inmost heart of the thing; detected the inmost mystery of it, namely the melody that lies hidden in it; the inward harmony of coherence which is its soul, whereby it exists, and has a right to be, here in this world. All inmost things, we may say, are melodious; naturally utter themselves in Song. The meaning of Song goes deep. Who is there that, in logical words, can express the effect music has on us? A kind of inarticulate unfathomable speech, which leads us to the edge of the Infinite, and lets us for moments gaze into that!

—THOMAS CARLYLE.
"The Hero as Poet." *On Heroes, Hero-Worship, and The Heroic in History.*

Orpheus with his lute made trees,
And the mountain tops that freeze,
Bow themselves when he did sing:
To his music plants and flowers
Ever sprung; as sun and showers
There had made a lasting spring.
Every thing that heard him play,
Even the billows of the sea,
Hung their heads, and then lay by.
In sweet music is such art,
Killing care and grief of heart
Fall asleep, or hearing, die.

—WILLIAM SHAKESPEARE.
"Orpheus." *Henry VIII.*

Yes; Music is the Memory of the heart;
And Memory is the Melody of love!—
How many dear affections around us start,
How many social pleasures do we prove,
When Music—like a Spirit from above—
Hallows the hour until it seems divine!—
When voices in melodious feeling move,
When Poesy and Harmony combine,
To soften and subdue—to gladden and refine!

—CHARLES SWAIN.
"The Mind." *The Mind, and Other Poems.*

Poetry and Music unite in song. From the earliest ages song has been the sweet companion of labor. The rude chant of the boatman floats upon the water, the shepherd sings upon the hill, the milkmaid in the dairy, the ploughman at the plough. Every trade, every occupation, every act and scene of life, has long had its own especial music. The bride went to her marriage, the laborer to his work, the old man to his last long rest, each with appropriate and immemorial music.

Music has been truly described as the mother of sympathy, the handmaid of Religion, and will never exercise its full effect, as the Emperor Charles VI said to Farinelli, unless it aims not merely to charm the ear, but to touch the heart.

—SIR JOHN LUBBOCK.
"Music." *The Pleasures of Life.*

O friend! this body is His lyre; He tightens its strings, and draws from it the melody of Brahma.

—Kabir.
Songs of Kabir.

When thou commandest me to sing it seems that my heart would break with pride; and I look to thy face, and tears come to my eyes. All that is harsh and dissonant in my life melts into one sweet harmony—and my adoration spreads wings like a glad bird on its flight across the sea. I know thou takest pleasure in my singing. I know that only as a singer I come before thy presence. I touch by the edge of the far-spreading wing of my song thy feet which I could never aspire to reach. Drunk with the joy of singing I forget myself and call thee friend who art my lord.

—Rabindranath Tagore.
Gitanjali (Song Offerings).

Where'er we turn, music is found,
With all its Heaven-born power to charm,
To lull us with its soothing sound,
And shed around a holy balm—
Pure as the thrilling, heavenly strains
From angels' harps, on Judah's plains.

Shall man, rescued from death and hell,
Shall he alone refuse to raise
His feeble voice, the song to swell
Unto his great Creator's praise?

While seraphs and archangels join
The blissful harmony divine.

—JAMES MONROE WHITFIELD.
"Ode To Music."

To priests and to prophets
The joy of their creeds,
To kings and their cohorts
The glory of deeds;
And peace to the vanquished
And hope to the strong. . . .
For me, O my Master,
The rapture of Song!

—SAROJINI NAIDU.
"Guerdon." *The Bird of Time.*
Songs of Life, Death & the Spring.

Part Three

ON CHARACTER, CONDUCT, VIRTUES

Chapter 19

On the Golden Mean, Moderation, Temperance, the Middle Way

And yet 'tis just the golden mean
That checks our lives' unsteady flow;
God's counterbalance thrown between,
To poise the scale 'twixt joy and woe:
And better so; for were the bowl
Too freely to the parched lip given,
Too much of grief would crush the soul,
Too much of joy would wean from heaven.

—Egbert Phelps.
"Life's Incongruities".

The flowers are at their best when they are half open; wine tastes the sweetest when the drinker is not too much intoxicated. The golden mean is all-important.

—Hung Ying-Ming.
Musings of a Chinese Vegetarian.

*There is nothing better than moderation
for teaching people or serving Heaven.
Those who use moderation
are already on the path to the Tao.*

—Lao-Tzu.
Tao Te Ching.

*Standing alone, in vale or mountain-top,
Upon the grassy plain, or ocean shore,
Or far away upon a ship at sea,
We are the middle of the Universe.
Around us as a centre, Earth and Heaven
Describe their mystic circles evermore.
We move; and all the radii shape themselves
To the one point and focus of our eyes.*

*But in our mental life we disobey
The law of circles: on the outer verge
We stand for ever, sometimes looking down
Upon extraneous evil far removed
Beyond the bound of Earth's circumference,
Adown dark tangents, infinitely stretched,
Through gloomy Chaos, troubled by Despair.*

*At other times we seek the sunniest verge,
The amber and the purple blooms of Heaven,
And strive with yearning eyes, made dim by tears,
To pierce the secrets of a happier state.
Exulting are we now, - and now forlorn.*

Lord grant us wisdom! grant that we may stand

In the fair middle of the spiritual world,
Undarken'd by the glooms of utter night,
Undazzled by the noontide glow of day.
True wisdom and serenity of soul
Dwell in the centre, and avoid extremes.

—CHARLES MACKAY.
"Serenity." *Voices from the Mountains and from the Crowd.*

There is nothing therefore in the world more wholesome or more necessary for us to learn, than this gracious lesson of moderation: .... This is the centre wherein all both divine and moral philosophy meet; the rule of life; the governess of manners; the silken string that runs through the pearl-chain of all virtues; the very ecliptic line under which reason and religion move without any deviation; and therefore most worthy of our best thoughts, our most careful observance.

—JOSEPH HALL.
Christian Moderation.

There is a limit to enjoyment, though the sources of wealth be boundless:
And the choicest pleasures of life lie within the ring of moderation.

—MARTIN FARQUHAR TUPPER.
"Of Compensation." *Proverbial Philosophy: A Book of Thoughts and Arguments.*

…. for truth, no less than virtue, not unfrequently forms the middle point between two extremes.

—CHARLES CALEB COLTON.
"Preface." *Lacon: Or, Many Things in Few Words; Addressed to Those who Think.*

Temperance is reason's girdle and passion's bridle; the strength of the soul and the foundation of virtue.

—JEREMY TAYLOR.
The Works of Jeremy Taylor D.D., Volume 1.

Nothing is good singly without its complement and its contrary. Self-examination is dangerous if it encroaches upon self-devotion; reverie is hurtful when it stupefies the will; gentleness is an evil when it lessens strength; contemplation is fatal when it destroys character. "Too much" and "too little" sin equally against wisdom. Excess is one evil, apathy another. Duty may be defined as energy tempered by moderation; happiness, as inclination calmed and tempered by self-control.

—HENRI-FRÉDÉRIC AMIEL.
Amiel's Journal. The Journal Intime of Henri-Frédéric Amiel.

To husband strength, mental and physical - to husband and govern power, passion, every impulse and every attribute of our nature, so that there may ever be with us the reserve-strength for use and enjoyment - is one of the chief secrets of happiness. Excess in pleasure or enjoyment is the bane of life. To stop a little short of the point of repletion is the golden secret.

—Prentice Mulford.
"Coarse Gold."

All virtues lie between
Excess and defect,
A narrow path betwixt
Hell's bottomless abyss,
Fine and sharp as a sword blade,
Which permits no lingering
Or turning round.
Equipoise is the summit of perfection,
Becoming like a simple essence.
As the rays of the sun
Shine upon the earth,
So the Light from the Spirit World
Shines brightly on him
Who has attained this equilibrium.

—Mahmud Shabistari.
"Part IX. Man: His Capabilities and His Destiny." *The Secret Rose Garden of Sa'd Ud Din Mahmud Shabistari.*

Chapter 20

ON GRATITUDE, THANKFULNESS

My heart gives thanks for many things;
I know not how to name them all.
My soul is free from frets and stings,
My mind from creed and doctrine's thrall,
For sun and stars, for flowers and streams,
For work and hope and rest and play—
For empty moments given to dreams,
For these my heart gives thanks to-day.

—WILLIAM STANLEY BRAITHWAITE.
"Thanksgiving." *Lyrics of Life and Love.*

Think not so much of what thou hast not as of what thou hast: but of the things which thou hast select the best, and then reflect how eagerly they would have been sought, if thou hadst them not. At the same time, however, take care that thou dost not through being so pleased with them accustom thyself to over- value them, so as to be disturbed if ever thou shouldst not have them.

—MARCUS AURELIUS.
The Meditations of Marcus Aurelius.

Be grateful for the kindly friends that walk along your way;
Be grateful for the skies of blue that smile from day to day;
Be grateful for the health you own, the work you find to do,
For round about you there are men less fortunate than you.

Be grateful for the growing trees, the roses soon to bloom,
The tenderness of kindly hearts that shared your days of gloom;
Be grateful for the morning dew, the grass beneath your feet,
The soft caresses of your babes and all their laughter sweet.

Acquire the grateful habit, learn to see how blest you are,
How much there is to gladden life, how little life to mar!
And what if rain shall fall to-day and you with grief are sad;
Be grateful that you can recall the joys that you have had.

—Edgar Albert Guest.
"Gratitude." *A Heap o' Living'.*

I am not rich in heaped stores of gold,
But other wealth I have to me more dear.
Not grand estates, but friends both new and old,
And memories of days long gone and near.

Not mines, but love of work, and robust health,
And joy in all the beauties of the earth,
A soul which thirsts for truth—eternal wealth.
Not rubies, but those gems of greater worth—
Belief in what the future has for me,
And faith to walk e'en where I cannot see.
My treasures these. Nor locks nor bars they need,
Nor care lest age or rust should dim or mar,
Not one excites the miser's lustful greed.

Ah, far better than gold my riches are!

—IDA LOUISE REVELEY.
"My Riches."

These are the things I prize
And hold of dearest worth:
Light of the sapphire skies,
Peace of the silent hills,
Shelter of forests, comfort of the grass,
Music of birds, murmur of little rills,
Shadow of clouds that swiftly pass,
And, after showers,
The smell of flowers
And of the good brown earth,—
And best of all, along the way, friendship and mirth.

—HENRY VAN DYKE.
"God of the Open Air."

Apart also from good that is public and many-voiced, does not each of us know, in private experience, much to be thankful for? Not only the innocent and daily pleasures that we have prized according to our wisdom; of the sun and starry skies, the fields of green, or snow scarcely less beautiful, the loaf eaten with an appetite, the glow of labor, the gentle signs of common affection; but have not some, have not many of us, cause to be thankful for enfranchisement from error or infatuation; a growth in knowledge of outward things, and instruction within the soul from a higher source. Have we not acquired a sense of more refined enjoyments; clear convictions; sometimes a serenity in which, as in the first days of June, all things grow, and the blossom gives place to fruit? Have we not been weaned from what was unfit for us, or unworthy our care? and have not those ties been drawn more close, and are not those objects seen more distinctly, which shall forever be worthy the purest desires of our souls? Have we learned to do any thing, the humblest, in the service and by the spirit of the power which meaneth all things well? If so, we may give thanks, and, perhaps, venture to offer our solicitations in behalf of those as yet less favored by circumstances. When even a few shall dare do so with the whole heart—for only a pure heart, can "avail much" in such prayers—then ALL shall soon be well.

—MARGARET FULLER OSSOLI.
"Thanksgiving." *Life Without and Life Within, Or, Reviews, Narratives, Essays, and Poems.*

For grief unsuffered, tears unshed,
For clouds that scattered overhead;
For pestilence that came not nigh,
For dangers great that passed us by;
For blood unspilled in wars unfought,
For deeds of shame and wrong unwrought;
For sharp suspicion, soothed, allayed,
For doubt dispelled that made afraid;
For fierce temptation well withstood,
For evil plot that brought forth good;
For weakened links in friendship's chain
That, sorely tested, stood the strain;

For harmless blows with malice dealt,
For base ingratitude unfelt;
For hatred's keen, unuttered word,
For bitter jest, unknown, unheard;
For every evil turned away,
Unmeasured thanks we give today.

—Rosalie May Cody.
"Thanksgiving." *In Flight.*

And, therefore, notwithstanding all that I have suffered, notwithstanding all the pain and weariness and anxiety and sorrow that necessarily enter into life, and the inward errings that are worse than all, I would end my record with a devout thanksgiving to the great Author of my being. For more and more am I unwilling to make my gratitude to him what is commonly called "a thanksgiving for mercies,"—for any benefits or blessings that are peculiar to myself, or my friends, or indeed to any man. Instead of this, I would have it to be gratitude for all that belongs to my life and being,— for joy and sorrow, for health and sickness, for success and disappointment, for virtue and for temptation, for life and death; because I believe that all is meant for good.

—Orville Dewey.
Autobiography and Letters of Orville Dewey, D.D.

On pleasure now, and now on vengeance bent,
The lab'ring passions struggle for a vent.
What pow'r, O man! thy reason then restores,
So long suspended in nocturnal hours?

What secret hand returns the mental train,
And gives improv'd thine active pow'rs again?
From thee, O man, what gratitude should rise!
And, when from balmy sleep thou op'st thine eyes,
Let thy first thoughts be praises to the skies.
How merciful our God who thus imparts
O'erflowing tides of joy to human hearts…

—PHILLIS WHEATLEY.
"Thoughts on the Works of Providence." *Poems on Various Subjects, Religious and Moral.*

Chapter 21

On Courage, Strength of Spirit

*Keep thy spirit pure
From worldly taint, by the repellent strength
Of virtue. Think on noble thoughts and deeds
Ever. Count o'er the rosary of truth,
And practise precepts which are proven wise.
It matters not, then, what thou fearest; walk
Boldly and fearlessly in the light thou hast;
There is a Hand above will lead thee on.*

—Philip James Bailey.
"Scene-A Village Feast-Evening." *Festus. A Poem.*

And truly it demands something godlike in him who has cast off the common motives of humanity and has ventured to trust himself for a taskmaster. High be his heart, faithful his will, clear his sight, that he may in good earnest be doctrine, society, law, to himself, that a simple purpose may be to him as strong as iron necessity is to others!

—Ralph Waldo Emerson.
"Self-Reliance." *Essays, First Series.*

Life is before ye—from the fated road
Ye cannot turn: then take ye up your load.
Not yours to tread, or leave the unknown way,
Ye must go o'er it, meet ye what ye may.
Gird up your souls within ye to the deed,
Angels, and fellow-spirits, bid ye speed!

A sacred burthen is this life ye bear,
Look on it, lift it, bear it solemnly,
Stand up and walk beneath it steadfastly;
Fail not for sorrow, falter not for sin,
But onward, upward, till the goal ye win;
God guard ye, and God guide ye on your way,
Young pilgrim warriors who set forth to-day!

—FRANCES ANNE BUTLER (LATE FANNY KEMBLE).
"Lines, Addressed to the Young Gentlemen leaving the Academy at Lennox, Massachusetts." *Poems.*

Press on! there's no such word as fail!
Press nobly on! the goal is near—
Ascend the mountain! breast the gale!
Look upward, onward—never fear!
Why should'st thou faint? Heaven smiles above
Though storm and vapor intervene;
That sun shines on, whose name is Love,
Serenely o'er Life's shadowed scene.
Press on! if Fortune play thee false
To-day, to-morrow she'll be true;
Whom now she sinks she now exalts,
Taking old gifts and granting new.
The wisdom of the present hour

Makes up for follies past and gone—
To weakness strength succeeds, and power
From frailty springs—press on! press on!

Therefore press on! and reach the goal
And gain the prize and wear the crown;
Faint not! for to the steadfast soul
Come wealth and honor and renown.
To thine own self be true, and keep
Thy mind from sloth, thy heart from soil:
Press on! and thou shalt surely reap
A heavenly harvest for thy toil!

—Park Benjamin.
"Press On."

The right use of Fate is to bring up our conduct to the loftiness of nature. Rude and invincible except by themselves are the elements. So let man be. Let him empty his breast of his windy conceits, and show his lordship by manners and deeds on the scale of nature. Let him hold his purpose as with the tug of gravitation. No power, no persuasion, no bribe shall make him give up his point. A man ought to compare advantageously with a river, an oak, or a mountain. He shall have not less the flow, the expansion, and the resistance of these.

'Tis the best use of Fate to teach a fatal courage. Go face the fire at sea, or the cholera in your friend's house, or the burglar in your own, or what danger lies in the way of duty, knowing you are guarded by the cherubim of Destiny. If you believe in Fate to your harm, believe it, at least, for your good.

—Ralph Waldo Emerson.
"Fate." *The Conduct of Life.*

I LIKE the man who faces what he must
With step triumphant and a heart of cheer;
Who fights the daily battle without fear;
Sees his hopes fail, yet keeps unfaltering trust
That God is God,—that somehow, true and just
His plans work out for mortals; not a tear
Is shed when fortune, which the world holds dear,
Falls from his grasp—better, with love, a crust
Than living in dishonor; envies not,
Nor loses faith in man; but does his best,
Nor ever murmurs at his humbler lot;
But, with a smile and words of hope, gives zest
To every toiler. He alone is great
Who by a life heroic conquers fate.

—SARAH KNOWLES BOLTON.
"The Inevitable."

As for myself, "I was bred to the plow." Amid the rugged hills, along the banks of Green River in Kentucky, I enjoyed the inestimable blessings of cabin life and hard work during the whole of my early days. I was in bondage,—*I never was a slave,*—the infamous laws of a savage despotism took my substance—what of that? Many a man has lost all he had, excepting his manhood. Adversity is the school of heroism, endurance the majesty of man and hope the torch of high aspirations. Acquainted with adversity, I am flattered of hope and comforted by endurance.

—ALBERY ALLSON WHITMAN.
"Dedicatory Address." *The Rape of Florida.*

Yea, you may quell my blood with sudden anguish,
Fetter my limbs with some compelling pain—
How will you daunt my free, far-journeying fancy
That rides upon the pinions of the rain?
How will you tether my triumphant mind,
Rival and fearless comrade of the wind?
Tho' you deny the hope of all my being,
Betray my love, my sweetest dream destroy,
Yet will I slake my individual sorrow
At the deep source of Universal joy—
O Fate, in vain you hanker to control
My frail, serene, indomitable soul.

—Sarojini Naidu.
"A Challenge to Fate." *The Bird of Time. Songs of Life,*
Death & the Spring.

Courage comes naturally to those who have the habit of facing labor and danger, and who therefore know the power of their arms and bodies; and courage or confidence in the mind comes to those who know by use its wonderful forces and inspirations and returns. Belief in its future is a reward kept only for those who use it.

—Ralph Waldo Emerson.
"Immortality."

I fight a battle every day
   Against discouragement and fear;
Some foe stands always in my way,
   The path ahead is never clear!

I must forever be on guard
  Against the doubts that skulk along;
I get ahead by fighting hard,
  But fighting keeps my spirit strong.

I have to fight my doubts away,
  And be on guard against my fears;
The feeble croaking of Dismay
  Has been familiar through the years;
My dearest plans keep going wrong,
  Events combine to thwart my will,
But fighting keeps my spirit strong,
  And I am undefeated still!

—SAMUEL ELLSWORTH KISER.
"The Fighter."

The human Will, that force unseen,
 The offspring of a deathless Soul,
 Can hew the way to any goal,
 Though walls of granite intervene.
Be not impatient in delay,
 But wait as one who understands;
When spirit rises and commands
The gods are ready to obey.

—ELLA WHEELER WILCOX.
"Will." *Poems of Power.*

Rise, soul, from thy despairing knees.
What if thy lips have drunk the lees?

Fling forth thy sorrows to the wind
And link thy hope with humankind—
The passion of a larger claim
Will put thy puny grief to shame.
Breathe the world thought, do the world deed,
Think hugely of thy brother's need.
And what thy woe, and what thy weal?
Look to the work the times reveal!
Give thanks with all thy flaming heart—
Crave but to have in it a part.
Give thanks and clasp thy heritage—
To be alive in such an age!

—Angela Morgan.
"Today."

O while I live to be the ruler of life, not a slave,
To meet life as a powerful conqueror,
No fumes, no ennui, no more complaints or scornful criticisms,
To these proud laws of the air, the water and the ground, proving my interior soul impregnable,
And nothing exterior shall ever take command of me.

—Walt Whitman.
"Song of Joys." *Leaves of Grass.*

OFT when the way I go lies hard and steep
Before me, and I cannot see my goal:
When those dream-kindled hopes wherewith my soul
Lighted the path have failed; when I could weep

To think how slow, unfirm a pace I keep,
How weak my faith, how slight my self-control,
Or will to speed me forward, though the whole
O'er-ripe world-harvest waits ahead to reap;
Oft in these hours I listen to the voice
Of seers and heroes through the ages past,
Who knew at length the metes and bounds of
fate,
And always, whatsoe'er their lot or choice,
One clear command they give: Or slow or fast,
Despair not, trust thyself, and trusting, wait.

—LESLIE PINCKNEY HILL.
"Nil Desperandum." *The Wings of Oppression.*

There is hope, but nothing of fear,
Nought but a patient mind,
For him who waits with conscience clear
And soul resigned
Whate'er the mystic coming change
Shall bring of new and strange.
He looks back once upon the fields of life,
The good and evil locked in strife,
The happy and the unhappy days,
The Right we always love, the oft-triumphant Wrong;
And all his being to a secret song
Sings with a mighty and unfaltering voice—
"I have been; Thou hast done all things well; I am
glad; I give thanks; I rejoice!"

—LEWIS MORRIS.
"The Ode of Change." *The Ode of Life.*

Chapter 22

On Non-Attachment, Detachment, Letting Go

When Heaven gives and takes away
can you be content with the outcome?
When you understand all things
can you step back from your own understanding?

Giving birth and nourishing,
making without possessing,
expecting nothing in return.
To grow, yet not to control:
This is the mysterious virtue.

—Lao-Tzu.
Tao Te Ching.

With equal mind, what happens, let us bear,
Nor joy, nor grieve too much for things beyond our care.

—John Dryden.
Palemon and Arcite; or the Knight's Tale from Chaucer, Book III.

Troublesome things must not be taken too seriously if they can be avoided. It is preposterous to take to heart that which you should throw over your shoulders. Much that would be something has become nothing by being left alone, and what was nothing has become of consequence by being made much of. At the outset things can be easily settled, but not afterwards. Often the remedy causes the disease. 'Tis by no means the least of life's rules: to let things alone.

—Baltasar Gracián.
The Art of Worldly Wisdom.

If thou workest at that which is before thee, following right reason seriously, vigorously, calmly, without allowing anything else to distract thee, but keeping thy divine part pure, as if thou shouldst be bound to give it back immediately; if thou holdest to this, expecting nothing, fearing nothing, but satisfied with thy present activity according to nature, and with heroic truth in every word and sound which thou utterest, thou wilt live happy. And there is no man who is able to prevent this.

—Marcus Aurelius.
The Meditations of Marcus Aurelius.

"Very well," replied the Spirit of the River, "am I then to regard the universe as great and the tip of a hair as small?"

"Not at all," said the Spirit of the Ocean. "Dimensions are limitless; time is endless. Conditions are not invariable; terms are not final. Thus, the wise man looks into space, and does not regard the small as too little, nor the great as too much; for he knows that there is no limit to dimension. He looks back into the past, and does not grieve over what is far off, nor rejoice over what is near; for he knows that time is without end.

He investigates fulness and decay, and does not rejoice if he succeeds, nor lament if he fails; for he knows that conditions are not invariable.

—Chuang Tzu.
Chuang Tzŭ. Mystic, Moralist, and Social Reformer.

One by one the sands are flowing,
One by one the moments fall:
Some are coming, some are going;
Do not strive to grasp them all.

One by one thy duties wait thee;
Let thy whole strength go to each;
Let no future dreams elate thee;
Learn thou first what these can teach.

One by one,—bright gifts of heaven,—
Joys are sent thee here below;
Take them readily when given;
Ready be to let them go.

—Adelaide Anne Procter.
"One by One." *The Poems of Adelaide A. Procter.*

Don't worry because things go against you. Don't be overjoyed because everything turns out as you wish them. Don't rely upon the permanency of happiness. Don't shrink from difficulties you may encounter at the outset of your enterprises.

—Hung Ying-Ming.
Musings of a Chinese Vegetarian.

Again, when fortune smiles and the stream of life flows according to our wishes, let us diligently avoid all arrogance, haughtiness, and pride. For it is as much a sign of weakness to give way to one's feelings in success as it is in adversity. But it is a fine thing to keep an unruffled temper, an unchanging mien, and the same cast of countenance in every condition of life.

—Marcus Tullius Cicero.
Cicero: de Officiis.

But thou, want not! ask not! Find full reward
Of doing right in right! Let right deeds be
Thy motive, not the fruit which comes from them.
And live in action! Labour! Make thine acts
Thy piety, casting all self aside,
Contemning gain and merit; equable
In good or evil: equability
Is Yog, is piety!

—The Bhagavad-Gita.

Chapter 23

ON HAPPINESS, CONTENTMENT

To happiness I raise my glass,
The goal of every human,
The hope of every clan and class
And every man and woman.
The daydreams of the urchin there,
The sweet theme of the maiden's prayer,
The strong man's one ambition,
The sacred prize of mothers sweet,
The tramp of soldiers on the street
Have all the selfsame mission.
Life here is nothing more or less
Than just a quest for happiness.

Some seek it on the mountain top,
And some within a mine;
The widow in her notion shop
Expects its sun to shine.
The tramp that seeks new roads to fare,
Is one with king and millionaire
In this that each is groping
On different roads, in different ways,
To come to glad, contented days,
And shares the common hoping.

The sound of martial fife and drum
Is born of happiness to come.

Yet happiness is always here
Had we the eyes to see it;
No breast but holds a fund of cheer
Had man the will to free it.
'Tis there upon the mountain top,
Or in the widow's notion shop,
'Tis found in homes of sorrow;
'Tis woven in the memories
Of happier, brighter days than these,
The gift, not of to-morrow
But of to-day, and in our tears
Some touch of happiness appears.

'Tis not a joy that's born of wealth:
The poor man may possess it.
'Tis not alone the prize of health:
No sickness can repress it.
'Tis not the end of mortal strife,
The sunset of the day of life,
Or but the old should find it;
It is the bond twixt God and man,
The touch divine in all we plan,
And has the soul behind it.
And so this toast to happiness,
The seed of which we all possess.

—Edgar Albert Guest.
"A Toast To Happiness." *A Heap o' Livin'*.

What then is human wisdom? Where is the path of true happiness? The mere limitation of our desires is not enough, for if they were less than our powers, part of our faculties would be idle, and we should not enjoy our whole being; neither is the mere extension of our powers enough, for if our desires were also increased we should only be the more miserable. True happiness consists in decreasing the difference between our desires and our powers, in establishing a perfect equilibrium between the power and the will. Then only, when all its forces are employed, will the soul be at rest and man will find himself in his true position.

—Jean-Jacques Rousseau.
Emile. Book II.

No one seems to doubt the immense human interest attached to joy. It is a sacred flame that must be fed, and that throws a splendid radiance over life. He who takes pains to foster it accomplishes a work as profitable for humanity as he who builds bridges, pierces tunnels, or cultivates the ground. So to order one's life as to keep, amid toils and suffering, the faculty of happiness, and be able to propagate it in a sort of salutary contagion among one's fellow-men, is to do a work of fraternity in the noblest sense. To give a trifling pleasure, smooth an anxious brow, bring a little light into dark paths—what a truly divine office in the midst of this poor humanity! But it is only in great simplicity of heart that one succeeds in filling it.

—Charles Wagner.
The Simple Life.

Someone notes that happiness and simplicity are old-time friends, and wiser words are rarely spoken. Happiness is found everywhere, but she prefers the common place—the quiet lane, the restful river, the simple toil and tool and task. She leans rather to the cottage than to the castle.

Good health, kind friends, encouraging words, loving deeds, duty done, heartaches healed, a grasp, a clasp, a kiss, a smile, a song, a welcome—these are the beams that bring summer into the soul and make us light-hearted and free and glad.

—MALCOLM JAMES MCLEOD.
"Simplicity and Happiness." *The Culture of Simplicity.*

If solid happiness we prize,
Within our breast this jewel lies,
And they are fools who roam;
The world hath nothing to bestow,
From our own selves our bliss must flow,
And that dear hut our home.

—NATHANIEL COTTON.
"The Fire-Side." *The Works of the British Poets: With Prefaces, Biographical and Critical, Volume 11.*

Happiness is the greatest paradox in Nature. It can grow in any soil, live under any conditions. It defies environment. It comes from within; it is the revelation of the depths of the inner life as light and heat proclaim the sun from which they radiate. Happiness consists not of having, but of being; not of possessing, but of enjoying. It is the warm glow of a heart at peace with itself.

The basis of happiness is the love of something outside self. Search every instance of happiness in the world, and you will find, when all the incidental features are eliminated, there is always the constant, unchangeable element of love,— love of parent for child; love of man and woman for each other; love of humanity in some form, or a great life work into which the individual throws all his energies.

—WILLIAM GEORGE JORDAN.
The Majesty of Calmness.

I found him seated on a bench before the door, smoking his pipe in the soft evening sunshine. .... How comforting it is to see a cheerful and contented old age, and to behold a poor fellow like this, after being tempest-tost through life, safely moored in a snug and quiet harbor in the evening of his days! His happiness, however, sprung from within himself and was independent of external circumstances, for he had that inexhaustible good-nature which is the most precious gift of Heaven, spreading itself like oil over the troubled sea of thought, and keeping the mind smooth and equable in the roughest weather.

—WASHINGTON IRVING.
"The Angler." *The Sketch Book of Geoffrey Crayon, Gent.*

Not that I speak in respect of want: for I have learned, in whatsoever state I am, therewith to be content.

—PHILIPPIANS 4:11. *KJV.*

That happiness does still the longest thrive,
Where joys and griefs have turns alternative.

—Robert Herrick.
"Happiness." *The Hesperides & Noble Numbers.*

Whoever I am, wherever my lot,
Whatever I happen to be,
Contentment and Duty shall hallow the spot
That Providence orders for me.

—Martin Farquhar Tupper.
"My Own Place."

My crown is in my heart, not on my head;
Not deck'd with diamonds, and Indian stones,
Nor to be seen: my crown is call'd Content;
A crown it is, that seldom kings enjoy.

—William Shakespeare.
Henry VI. Part 3.

Where grows?—where grows it not? If vain our toil,
We ought to blame the culture, not the soil:
Fixed to no spot is happiness sincere,
'Tis nowhere to be found, or everywhere;
'Tis never to be bought, but always free,
And fled from monarchs, St. John! dwells with thee.

—Alexander Pope.
"Epistle IV." *An Essay on Man. Moral Essays and Satires.*

Chapter 24

ON SORROWS AND JOYS

Let no man pray that he know not sorrow,
Let no soul ask to be free from pain,
For the gall of to-day is the sweet of to-morrow,
And the moment's loss is the lifetime's gain.
Through want of a thing does its worth redouble,
Through hunger's pangs does the feast content,
And only the heart that has harbored trouble,
Can fully rejoice when joy is sent.
Let no man shrink from the bitter tonics
Of grief, and yearning, and need, and strife,
For the rarest chords in the soul's harmonies,
Are found in the minor strains of life.

—ELLA WHEELER WILCOX.
"Life's Harmonies". *Poems of Power.*

Upon the sadness of the sea
The sunset broods regretfully;
From the far, lonely spaces, slow
Withdraws the wistful afterglow.
So out of life the splendor dies;
So darken all the happy skies;
So gathers twilight, cold and stern;

But overhead the planets burn.
And up the east another day
Shall chase the bitter dark away;
What though our eyes with tears be wet?
The sunrise never failed us yet.
The blush of dawn may yet restore
Our light and hope and joy once more;
Sad soul, take comfort, nor forget
That sunrise never failed us yet.

—Celia Thaxter.
"The Sunrise Never Failed Us Yet."
The Poems of Celia Thaxter.

At bottom, the world is to be interpreted in terms of joy, but of a joy that includes all the pain, includes it and transforms it and transcends it.

—Felix Adler.
Life and Destiny: Or, Thoughts from the Ethical Lectures of Felix Adler.

Nay, do not grieve tho' life be full of sadness,
Dawn will not veil her splendour for your grief,
Nor spring deny their bright, appointed beauty
To lotus blossom and ashoka leaf.

Nay, do not pine, tho' life be dark with trouble,
Time will not pause or tarry on his way;
To-day that seems so long, so strange, so bitter,
Will soon be some forgotten yesterday.

Nay, do not weep; new hopes, new dreams, new faces,
The unspent joy of all the unborn years,
Will prove your heart a traitor to its sorrow,
And make your eyes unfaithful to their tears.

—SAROJINI NAIDU.
"Transience." *The Bird of Time. Songs of Life, Death & the Spring.*

COUNT each affliction, whether light or grave,
God's messenger sent down to thee; do thou
With courtesy receive him; rise and bow;
Then lay before him all thou hast; allow
No cloud of passion to usurp thy brow,
Or mar thy hospitality; no wave
Of mortal tumult to obliterate
The soul's marmoreal calmness: Grief should be,
Like joy, majestic, equable, sedate;
Confirming, cleansing, raising, making free;
Strong to consume small troubles; to commend
Great thoughts, grave thoughts, thoughts lasting to the end.

—AUBREY DE VERE.
"Sorrow."

Suffering is doubtless as divinely appointed as joy, while it is much more influential as a discipline of character. It chastens and sweetens the nature, teaches patience and resignation, and promotes the deepest as well as the most exalted thought.

Life, all sunshine without shade, all happiness without sorrow, all pleasure without pain, were not life at all—at least not human life. Take the lot of the happiest—it is a tangled yarn. It is made up of sorrows and joys; and the joys are all the sweeter because of the sorrows; bereavements and blessings, one following another, making us sad and blessed by turns.

—SAMUEL SMILES.
"Chapter XII. The Discipline of Experience." *Character.*

My name is Sorrow—I shall come to all
To block the surfeit of an endless joy;
Along the Sable Road I pay my call
Before the sweetness of success can cloy;
And weaker souls shall weep amid the throng
And fall before me, broken and dismayed;
But braver hearts shall know that I belong
And take me in, serene and unafraid.

—GRANTLAND RICE.
"The Trainers" *Songs of the Stalwart.*

Do not cheat thy Heart and tell her
"Grief will pass away,
Hope for fairer times in future,
And forget to-day."—
Tell her if you will, that sorrow
Need not come in vain;
Tell her that the lesson taught her
Far outweighs the pain.

Rather bid her go forth bravely,
And the stranger greet;
Not as foe, with spear and buckler,
But as dear friends meet;
Bid her with a strong clasp hold her,
By her dusky wings,
Listening for the murmured blessing
Sorrow always brings.

—ADELAIDE ANNE PROCTER.
"Friend Sorrow." *The Poems of Adelaide A. Procter.*

When you are joyous, look deep into your heart and you shall find it is only that which has given you sorrow that is giving you joy.
When you are sorrowful look again in your heart, and you shall see that in truth you are weeping for that which has been your delight.
Some of you say, "Joy is greater than sorrow," and others say, "Nay, sorrow is the greater."
But I say unto you, they are inseparable.
Together they come, and when one sits alone with you at your board, remember that the other is asleep upon your bed.
Verily you are suspended like scales between your sorrow and your joy.

—KAHLIL GIBRAN.
The Prophet.

Love, hope, and joy, fair pleasure's smiling train,
Hate, fear, and grief, the family of pain,

These mixed with art, and to due bounds confined,
Make and maintain the balance of the mind;
The lights and shades, whose well-accorded strife
Gives all the strength and colour of our life.

—ALEXANDER POPE.
An Essay On Man. Moral Essays and Satires.

The world is overcome—aye! even here!
By such as fix their faith on Unity.
The sinless Brahma dwells in Unity,
And they in Brahma. Be not over-glad
Attaining joy, and be not over-sad
Encountering grief, but, stayed on Brahma, still
Constant let each abide!

—THE BHAGAVAD-GITA.

Chapter 25

On Giving, Charity, Generosity

The Tao works to use the excess,
and gives to that which is depleted.
The way of people is to take from the depleted,
and give to those who already have an excess.

Who is able to give to the needy from their excess?
Only someone who is following the way of the Tao.

This is why the Master gives
expecting nothing in return.
She does not dwell on her past accomplishments,
and does not glory in any praise.

—Lao-Tzu.
Tao Te Ching.

Honour the Lord with thy substance, and with the firstfruits of all thine increase:
So shall thy barns be filled with plenty, and thy presses shall burst out with new wine.

—Proverbs 3:9-10. *KJV.*

Then said a rich man, Speak to us of Giving.
And he answered:
You give but little when you give of your possessions.
It is when you give of yourself that you truly give.

It is well to give when asked, but it is better to give unasked,
through understanding;
And to the open-handed the search for one who shall
receive is joy greater than giving.
And is there aught you would withhold?
All you have shall some day be given;
Therefore give now, that the season of giving may be yours
and not your inheritors'.

—Kahlil Gibran.
The Prophet.

However meagre be my worldly wealth,
  Let me give something that shall aid my kind—
A word of courage, or a thought of health,
  Dropped as I pass for troubled hearts to find.
Let me to-night look back across the span
  'Twixt dawn and dark, and to my conscience say—
Because of some good act to beast or man—
  "The world is better that I lived to-day."

—Ella Wheeler Wilcox.
"Morning Prayer." Poems of Power.

Give, and it shall be given unto you; good measure, pressed down, and shaken together, and running over, shall men give into your bosom. For with the same measure that ye mete withal it shall be measured to you again.

—Luke 6:38. *KJV.*

I built a chimney for a comrade old;
   I did the service not for hope of hire:
And then I travelled on in winter's cold
   Yet all the day I glowed before the fire.

—Edwin Markham.
"Two at a Fireside." *The Man with the Hoe And Other Poems.*

Who gives and hides the giving hand,
Nor counts on favor, fame, or praise,
Shall find his smallest gift outweighs
The burden of the sea and land.

Who gives to whom hath naught been given,
His gift in need, though small indeed
As is the grass-blade's wind-blown seed,
Is large as earth and rich as heaven.

—John Greenleaf Whittier.
"Giving and Taking." *The Poetical Works of John Greenleaf Whittier.*

True generosity is a duty as indispensably necessary as those imposed upon us by the law. It is a rule imposed upon us by reason, which should be the sovereign law of a rational being.

—OLIVER GOLDSMITH.
"On Justice and Generosity." *The Miscellaneous Works of Oliver Goldsmith, M.B.*

And now abideth faith, hope, charity, these three; but the greatest of these is charity.

—1 CORINTHIANS 13:13. *KJV.*

To give of the fruits of one's labor to others is to contribute to the welfare of all men.

—COUNT LEO TOLSTOI.
My Religion.

It is more blessed to give than to receive.

—ACTS 20:35. *KJV.*

Oh, the blessedness of giving! How it enlarges our hearts and sweetens our toil to share our bounty with others!

It is the sweetness of silent alms that gladdens the heart of the Master and enriches the heart of the giver.

—IDA SCOTT TAYLOR.
"January Fifteenth." *The Year Book of English Authors.*

Give, it is like God; thou weariest the bad with benefits:
Give, it is like God; thou gladdenest the good by gratitude.

Give, saith the preacher, be large in liberality, yield to the holy impulse,
Tarry not for cold consideration, but cheerfully and freely scatter.

—Martin Farquhar Tupper.
"Of Gifts." *Proverbial Philosophy:*
A Book of Thoughts and Arguments.

So in life, we get by giving; we grow rich by scattering.

—James Allen.
Above Life's Turmoil.

For the heart grows rich in giving;
All its wealth is living grain;
Seeds which mildew in the garner,
Scattered, fill with gold the plain.

—Elizabeth Rundle Charles.
"The Cruse That Faileth Not."

Chapter 26

On Duty, Service

The highest duties oft are found
Lying on the lowest ground,
In hidden and unnoticed ways,
In household works, on common days.

—John S. B. Monsell.
Spiritual Songs for the Sundays and Holydays
Throughout the Year.

Now, while in the great encounters our equipment is generally adequate, it is precisely in the little emergencies that we are found wanting. Without fear of being misled by a paradoxical form of thought, I affirm, then, that the essential thing is to fulfil our simple duties and exercise elementary justice. In general, those who lose their souls do so not because they fail to rise to difficult duty, but because they neglect to perform that which is simple.

Often a man has not the means to do good on a large scale, but that is not a reason for failing to do it at all. So many people absolve themselves from any action, on the ground that there is too much to do! They should be recalled to simple duty, and this duty in the case of which we speak is that each one, according to his resources, leisure and capacity, should create relations for himself among the world's disinherited.

>   —Charles Wagner.
>   *The Simple Life.*

This does not mean that duty always is easy; it does not deny the self-sacrifice which right living involves. Everything worth while in the intellectual or moral life must be bought and paid for by giving up irreconcilable habits and indulgences.

>   —Harry Emerson Fosdick.
>   *Twelve Tests of Character.*

Thy sum of duty let two words contain,
(O may they graven in thy heart remain!)
Be humble and be just.

>   —Matthew Prior.
>   *Solomon on the Vanity of the World.*
>   *A Poem. In Three Books.*

For unto whomsoever much is given, of him shall be much required.

>   —Luke 12:48. *KJV.*

Man cannot get away from facts—
Alas, stern duty looms supreme,
For certain things we must perform,

Obey the inward voices' call.
Calm joyous days cannot be wooed
Unless our conscience is at peace.

—Sadakichi Hartmann.
My Rubaiyat.

We ought not to picture Duty to ourselves, or to others, as a stern taskmistress. She is rather a kind and sympathetic mother, ever ready to shelter us from the cares and anxieties of this world, and to guide us in the paths of peace.

To shut oneself up from mankind is, in most cases, to lead a dull, as well as a selfish life. Our duty is to make ourselves useful, and thus life may be most interesting, and yet comparatively free from anxiety.

—Sir John Lubbock.
"The Happiness of Duty." *The Pleasures of Life, Part I and Part II.*

Although philosophy offers many problems, both important and useful, that have been fully and carefully discussed by philosophers, those teachings which have been handed down on the subject of moral duties seem to have the widest practical application. For no phase of life, whether public or private, whether in business or in the home, whether one is working on what concerns oneself alone or dealing with another, can be without its moral duty; on the discharge of such duties depends all that is morally right, and on their neglect all that is morally wrong in life.

—Marcus Tullius Cicero.
Cicero: de Officiis.

Straight is the line of duty;
Curved is the line of beauty;
Follow the straight line, thou shalt see
The curved line ever follow thee.

—William MacCall.
"Duty."

Duty thus becomes our principle of action, our source of energy, the guarantee of our partial independence of the world, the condition of our dignity, the sign of our nobility. The world can neither make me will nor make me will my duty; here I am my own and only master, and treat with it as sovereign with sovereign. It holds my body in its clutches; but my soul escapes and braves it. My thought and my love, my faith and my hope, are beyond its reach. My true being, the essence of my nature, myself, remain inviolate and inaccessible to the world's attacks

—Henri-Frédéric Amiel.
Amiel's Journal: The Journal Intime of Henri-Frédéric Amiel.

The abiding sense of duty is the very crown of character.

Duty is based upon a sense of justice—justice inspired by love, which is the most perfect form of goodness. Duty is not a sentiment, but a principle pervading the life: and it exhibits itself in conduct and in acts…

—Samuel Smiles.
"Chapter VII. Duty—Truthfulness." *Character.*

Stern Daughter of the Voice of God!
O Duty! if that name thou love
Who art a light to guide, a rod
To check the erring, and reprove;
Thou, who art victory and law
When empty terrors overawe;
From vain temptations dost set free;
And calm'st the weary strife of frail humanity!

—WILLIAM WORDSWORTH.
"Ode to Duty." *Poems of Wordsworth.*

Accuse not Nature, she hath done her part;
Do thou but thine…

—JOHN MILTON.
"Book VIII." *Paradise Lost.*

For knowledge is a steep which few may climb,
While duty is a path which all may tread

—LEWIS MORRIS.
The Epic of Hades: In Three Books.

Mencius said. "Benevolence is the distinguishing characteristic of man. As embodied in man's conduct, it is called the path of duty."

—MENCIUS.
"Book VII. Tsin Sin. Part II." *The Chinese Classics: Vol. II containing The Works of Mencius.*

Whate'er thy race or speech, thou art the same;
Before thy eyes, Duty, a constant flame,
Shines always steadfast with unchanging light,
Through dark days and through bright.

—LEWIS MORRIS.
"The Ode of Perfect Years." *The Ode of Life.*

Go on in all simplicity; do not be so anxious to win a quiet mind, and it will be all the quieter. Do not examine so closely into the progress of your soul. Do not crave so much to be perfect, but let your spiritual life be formed by your duties, and by the actions which are called forth by circumstances.

—ST. FRANCIS DE SALES.
A Selection from the Spiritual Letters of s. Francis de Sales.

The sphere of Duty is infinite. It exists in every station of life. We have it not in our choice to be rich or poor, to be happy or unhappy; but it becomes us to do the duty that everywhere surrounds us. Obedience to duty, at all costs and risks, is the very essence of the highest civilised life.

—SAMUEL SMILES.
Duty: With Illustrations of Courage, Patience and Endurance.

….. it is no less incumbent on you to move steadily in the path of duty; for your active exertions are due not only to society, but in humble gratitude to the Being who made you a member of it, with powers to serve yourself and others.

—Sir Walter Scott.
The Waverley Novels. The Antiquary.

Don't do right unwillingly,
And stop to plan and measure;
'Tis working with the heart and soul
That makes our duty pleasure.

—Phoebe Cary.
"Now." *The Poetical Works of Alice and Phoebe Cary.*

Chapter 27

On Virtue and Virtues

Enquirer, cease, Petitions yet remain,
Which Heav'n may hear, nor deem Religion vain.
Still raise for Good the supplicating Voice,
But leave to Heav'n the Measure and the Choice.
Safe in his Pow'r, whose Eyes discern afar
The secret Ambush of a specious Pray'r.
Implore his Aid, in his Decisions rest,
Secure whate'er he gives, he gives the best.
Yet with the Sense of sacred Presence prest,
When strong Devotion fills thy glowing Breast,
Pour forth thy Fervours for a healthful Mind,
Obedient Passions, and a Will resign'd;
For Love, which scarce collective Man can fill;
For Patience sov'reign o'er transmuted Ill;
For Faith, that panting for a happier Seat,
Thinks Death kind Nature's Signal of Retreat:
These Goods for Man the Laws of Heav'n ordain,
These Goods he grants, who grants the Pow'r to gain;
With these celestial Wisdom calms the Mind,
And makes the Happiness she does not find.

—Samuel Johnson.
The Vanity of Human Wishes: The Tenth Satire of
Juvenal, Imitated by Samuel Johnson.

Virtue is that perfect good which is the complement of a happy life; the only immortal thing that belongs to mortality—it is the knowledge both of others and itself—it is an invincible greatness of mind, not to be elevated or dejected with good or ill fortune. It is sociable and gentle, free, steady, and fearless, content within itself, full of inexhaustible delights, and it is valued for itself.

—Lucius Annaeus Seneca.
"Of a Happy Life."

Let us be true: this is the highest maxim of art and of life, the secret of eloquence and of virtue, and of all moral authority.

—Henri-Frédéric Amiel.
Amiel's Journal. The Journal Intime of Henri-Frédéric Amiel.

Virtue and equity,
Courage and temperance,
Are the four qualities of the sage.
He is not over-cunning or a fool,
His appetites are under control,
From cringing and boasting he is free,
And from foolhardiness and cowardice.
All virtues lie between
Excess and defect,
A narrow path betwixt
Hell's bottomless abyss,
Fine and sharp as a sword blade,
Which permits no lingering

Or turning round.
Equipoise is the summit of perfection,
Becoming like a simple essence.
As the rays of the sun
Shine upon the earth,
So the Light from the Spirit World
Shines brightly on him
Who has attained this equilibrium.

—MAHMUD SHABISTARI.
"Part IX. Man: His Capabilities and His Destiny." *The Secret Rose Garden of Sa'd Ud Din Mahmud Shabistari.*

But where is the reward of virtue? And what recompense has nature provided for such important sacrifices, as those of life and fortune, which we must often make to it? Oh, sons of earth! Are ye ignorant of the value of this celestial mistress? And do ye meanly enquire for her portion, when ye observe her genuine charms? But know, that nature has been indulgent to human weakness, and has not left this favourite child, naked and unendowed. She has provided virtue with the richest dowry; but being careful, lest the allurements of interest should engage such suitors, as were insensible of the native worth of so divine a beauty, she has wisely provided, that this dowry can have no charms but in the eyes of those who are already transported with the love of virtue.

—DAVID HUME.
"Essay 16: The Stoic." *Essays Moral, Political, and Literary, Volume 1.*

Rouse thyself! do not be idle! Follow the law of virtue! The virtuous rests in bliss in this world and in the next.

Follow the law of virtue; do not follow that of sin. The virtuous rests in bliss in this world and in the next.

—*The Dhammapada.*

The sentiment of virtue is a reverence and delight in the presence of certain divine laws. It perceives that this homely game of life we play, covers, under what seem foolish details, principles that astonish. The child amidst his baubles, is learning the action of light, motion, gravity, muscular force; and in the game of human life, love, fear, justice, appetite, man, and God, interact. These laws refuse to be adequately stated. They will not be written out on paper, or spoken by the tongue. They elude our persevering thought; yet we read them hourly in each other's faces, in each other's actions, in our own remorse. The moral traits which are all globed into every virtuous act and thought,—in speech, we must sever, and describe or suggest by painful enumeration of many particulars.

—Ralph Waldo Emerson.
The Divinity School Address.

They have not grasped the whole truth who see in the sympathetic side of human nature, in the tender and amiable impulses of the heart, the well-spring of our moral judgments. These gentle qualities—pity, tenderness, sympathy—are the sweet, younger sisters of Virtue; but Virtue herself is greater than they.

—FELIX ADLER.
Life and Destiny: Or, Thoughts from the Ethical Lectures of Felix Adler.

Virtue is the health of the soul. It gives a flavour to the smallest leaves of life.

—JOSEPH JOUBERT.
"Of Wisdom, Virtue, and Morality." *Pensées of Joubert.*

Know, then, this truth (enough for man to know)
"Virtue alone is happiness below."
The only point where human bliss stands still,
And tastes the good without the fall to ill;
Where only merit constant pay receives,
Is blest in what it takes, and what it gives;
The joy unequalled, if its end it gain,
And if it lose, attended with no pain;
Without satiety, though e'er so blessed,
And but more relished as the more distressed:
The broadest mirth unfeeling folly wears,
Less pleasing far than virtue's very tears:
Good, from each object, from each place acquired
For ever exercised, yet never tired;
Never elated, while one man's oppressed;

Never dejected while another's blessed;
And where no wants, no wishes can remain,
Since but to wish more virtue, is to gain.

—ALEXANDER POPE.
"Epistle IV." *An Essay on Man. Moral Essays and Satires.*

Neither can it be said, on the other hand, that the gain of rectitude must be bought by any loss. There is no penalty to virtue; no penalty to wisdom; they are proper additions of being. In a virtuous action, I properly am; in a virtuous act, I add to the world; I plant into deserts conquered from Chaos and Nothing, and see the darkness receding on the limits of the horizon. There can be no excess to love; none to knowledge; none to beauty, when these attributes are considered in the purest sense. The soul refuses limits, and always affirms an Optimism, never a Pessimism.

—RALPH WALDO EMERSON.
"Compensation." *Essays, First Series.*

There is but one pursuit in life which it is in the power of all to follow, and of all to attain. It is subject to no disappointments, since he that perseveres, makes every difficulty an advancement, and every contest a victory; and this is the pursuit of virtue. Sincerely to aspire after virtue, is to gain her, and zealously to labour after her wages, is to receive them.

—CHARLES CALEB COLTON.
"XLIX." *Lacon: Or, Many Things in Few Words;*
Addressed to Those who Think.

Heaven doth with us as we with torches do;
Not light them for themselves; for if our virtues
Did not go forth of us, 'twere all alike
As if we had them not.

—WILLIAM SHAKESPEARE.
Measure for Measure.

Chapter 28

ON TALKING, SPEECH, WORDS

Even though a speech be a thousand, but made up of senseless words, one word of sense is better, which if a man hears, he becomes quiet.

Even though a Gâthâ be a thousand, but made up of senseless words, one word of a Gâthâ is better, which if a man hears, he becomes quiet.

Though a man recite a hundred Gâthâs made up of senseless words, one word of the law is better, which if a man hears, he becomes quiet.

—*The Dhammapada.*

I never, with important air,
In conversation overbear.
Can grave and formal pass for wise,
When men the solemn owl despise?
My tongue within my lips I rein;
For who talks much must talk in vain,
We from the wordy torrent fly:
Who listens to the chatt'ring pye?

—John Gay.
"The Shepherd and the Philosopher." *The Poetical Works of John Gay.*

Yet spurn not words! 'tis needful to confess
They give ideas, a body and a dress!
Behold them traverse Learning's region round,
The vehicles of thought on wheels of sound.

—Elizabeth Barrett Browning.
"An Essay on Mind." *An Essay on Mind, with Other Poems.*

Wherever men congregate, words are used. Man is born with the faculty of speech. Who gives it (to) him? He who gives the bird its song.

—Joseph Joubert.
"Of the Human Faculties." *Pensées of Joubert.*

If thou speakest not I will fill my heart with thy silence and endure it. I will keep still and wait like the night with starry vigil and its head bent low with patience.
The morning will surely come, the darkness will vanish, and thy voice pour down in golden streams breaking through the sky. Then thy words will take wing in songs from every one of my birds' nests, and thy melodies will break forth in flowers in all my forest groves.

—Rabindranath Tagore.
Gitanjali (Song Offerings).

All seed-sowing is a mysterious thing, whether the seed fall into the earth or into souls. Man is a husbandman; his whole work rightly understood is to develop life, to sow it everywhere. Such is the mission of humanity, and of this divine mission the great instrument is speech. We forget too often that language is both a seed-sowing and a revelation. The influence of a word in season, is it not incalculable? What a mystery is speech!

—Henri-Frédéric Amiel.
Amiel's Journal. The Journal Intime of Henri-Frédéric Amiel.

Some words are played on golden strings,
Which I so highly rate,
I cannot bear for meaner things
Their sound to desecrate.

For every day they are not meet,
Or for a careless tone;
They are for rarest, and most sweet,
And noblest use alone.

Trust me, the worth of words is such
They guard all noble things,
And that this rash irreverent touch
Has jarred some golden strings.

For what the lips have lightly said
The heart will lightly hold,
And things on which we daily tread
Are lightly bought and sold.

The sun of every day will bleach
The costliest purple hue.
And so our common daily speech
Discolours what was true.

But as you keep some thoughts apart
In sacred honoured care,
If in the silence of your heart,
Their utterance too be rare;

Then, while a thousand words repeat
Unmeaning clamours all,
Melodious golden echoes sweet
Shall answer when you call.

—Adelaide Anne Procter.
"Golden Words." *The Poems of Adelaide A. Procter.*

Speak gently!—It is better far
To rule by love, than fear—
Speak gently—let not harsh words mar
The good we might do here!

Speak gently!—Love doth whisper low
The vows that true hearts bind;
And gently Friendship's accents flow;
Affection's voice is kind.

Speak gently!—'t is a little thing
Dropped in the heart's deep well;
The good, the joy, which it may bring,
Eternity shall tell.

—David Bates.
"Speak Gently." *The Eolian.*

With what care should we guard our tongues, that they speak no ill, that they carry no sting, and that they always find an opportunity to say a word "in due season."

—Ida Scott Taylor.
"January Fifth." *The Year Book of English Authors.*

A word fitly spoken is like apples of gold in pictures of silver.

—Proverbs 25:11. *KJV.*

Chapter 29

ON SILENCE

*In silence was the Universe conceived,
In silence doth the heart of man seek out
That other heart to rest on; Nature's soul
Yearns ceaselessly to give its speechless calm
Unto her restless children as they roam
Far from that central place which is their home.*

*Wouldst know thy Mother Nature face to face?
Wouldst hear her silent heartbeats? Close thine ears
And still thy senses; wouldst thou feel her arms
Enfold thy being? Thou must give thyself
In uttermost abandon to her will
That she may teach thee the one truth—be still!*

*Be still—and from the Silences shall arise
A mem'ry of forgotten mysteries.
A healing peace descending on thy soul
Shall bear it up to regions beyond words
Where thou shalt learn the secrets of the earth.
Of wind and flame and how the stars have birth.*

—M. FRANCES POILE.
"Silence."

*Three Silences there are: the first of speech,
  The second of desire, the third of thought;*

This is the lore a Spanish monk, distraught
With dreams and visions, was the first to teach.
These Silences, commingling each with each,
Made up the perfect Silence, that he sought
And prayed for, and wherein at times he caught
Mysterious sounds from realms beyond our reach.

—HENRY WADSWORTH LONGFELLOW.
"The Three Silences of Molinos. To John Greenleaf Whittier." *Keramos and Other Poems.*

There are three kinds of Silence; the first is of Words, the second of Desires, and the third of Thoughts. The first is perfect; the second more perfect; and the third most perfect. In the first, that is, of Words, Virtue is acquired; in the second, to wit, of Desires, quietness is attained to; in the third of Thoughts, Internal Recollection is gained.

—MICHAEL (OR MIGUEL) DE MOLINOS.
"Of Internal and Mystical Silence." *The Spiritual Guide.*

SILENCE! *coeval with Eternity,*
Thou wert ere Nature's self began to be,
'T was one vast nothing all, and all slept fast in thee.

Thine was the sway ere Heav'n was form'd, or earth,
Ere fruitful thought conceiv'd Creation's birth,

—ALEXANDER POPE.
"Early Poems: Imitations of English Poets. Earl of Rochester: On Silence." *The Complete Poetical Works of Alexander Pope.*

What a strange power there is in silence! How many resolutions are formed—how many sublime conquests effected—during that pause when the lips are closed, and the soul secretly feels the eye of her Maker upon her!

They are the strong ones of the earth, the mighty food for good or evil,—those who know how to keep silence when it is a pain and a grief to them; those who give time to their own souls to wax strong against temptation, or to the powers of wrath to stamp upon them their withering passage.

—Lady Georgiana Fullerton.
Grantley Manor: A Tale.

But ye, keep ye on earth
Your lips from over-speech,
Loud words and longing are so little worth;
And the end is hard to reach.
For silence after grievous things is good,
And reverence, and the fear that makes men whole,
And shame, and righteous governance of blood,
And lordship of the soul.
But from sharp words and wits men pluck no fruit,
And gathering thorns they shake the tree at root;
For words divide and rend;
But silence is most noble till the end.

—Algernon Charles Swinburne.
Atalanta in Calydon: A Tragedy.

Down through the starry intervals,
Upon this weary-laden world,
How soft the soul of Silence falls!
How deep the spell wherewith she thralls;
How wide her mantle is unfurled!

She broods o'er the bewildering street:
Lo, day's turmoil and strivings cease;
She folds in sleep its rushing feet;
On traffic, racing loud and fleet,
She sets the signet of her peace.

—MARY CLEMMER.
"Silence." *Poems of Life and Nature.*

Chapter 30

ON SERENITY, INNER PEACE, EQUANIMITY, TRANQUILITY

*If one
Ponders on objects of the sense, there springs
Attraction; from attraction grows desire,
Desire flames to fierce passion, passion breeds
Recklessness; then the memory—all betrayed—
Lets noble purpose go, and saps the mind,
Till purpose, mind, and man are all undone.
But, if one deals with objects of the sense
Not loving and not hating, making them
Serve his free soul, which rests serenely lord,
Lo! such a man comes to tranquillity;
And out of that tranquillity shall rise
The end and healing of his earthly pains,
Since the will governed sets the soul at peace.*

—THE BHAGAVAD-GITA.

Then he returned to the window, and saw that the sun had gone quite down behind the window. And there came on the twilight of an August evening. And his soul grew calm with it; and it felt religious to him. And he said to himself, "Never, never do great thoughts come to a man while he is discontented or fretful. There must be quiet in the temple of his soul, before the windows of it will open for him to see out of them into the infinite. Quiet is what heavenly powers move in. It is in silence the stars move on; and it is in quiet our souls are visited from on high."

—William Mountford.
Thorpe: A Quiet English Town, and Human Life Therein.

Not in rewards, but in the strength to strive,
The blessing lies, and new experience gained;
In daily duties done, hope kept alive,
That Love and Thought are housed and entertained.

So not in vain the struggle, though the prize
Awaiting me was other than it seemed.
My feet have missed the paths of Paradise,
Yet life is even more blessed than I deemed.

Riches I never sought, and have not found,
And Fame has passed me with averted eye;
In creeks and bays my quiet voyage is bound,
While the great world without goes surging by.

No withering envy of another's lot,
Nor nightmare of contention, plagues my rest:
For me alike what is and what is not,
Both what I have and what I lack are best.

A flower more sacred than far-seen success
Perfumes my solitary path; I find
Sweet compensation in my humbleness,
And reap the harvest of a tranquil mind.

—JOHN TOWNSEND TROWBRIDGE.
"Twoscore and Ten."

.... for it is in thy power whenever thou shalt choose to retire into thyself. For nowhere either with more quiet or more freedom from troubles does a man retire than into his own soul, particularly when he has within him such thoughts that by looking into them he is immediately in perfect tranquility; and I affirm that tranquility is nothing else than the good ordering of the mind. Constantly then give to thyself this retreat, and renew thyself; and let thy principles be brief and fundamental, which, as soon as thou shalt recur to them, will be sufficient to cleanse the soul completely, and to send thee back free from all discontent with the things to which thou returnest.

—MARCUS AURELIUS.
The Meditations of Marcus Aurelius.

A second mark of the higher life is Serenity, and there is perhaps no surer sign by which exalted natures can be known. To be serene under all circumstances whatsoever, even in moments of imminent peril, in times of sudden reversal of fortune, of grievous personal loss or of public calamity, is the unmistakable badge of moral ripeness. But is it possible to preserve one's serenity in the supreme trials of life? It is possible, I should answer, if we have formed the habit of asking on every occasion. What is it right to do now? The habit of fixing our attention on how we are to conduct ourselves, on what, in a given situation and quite apart from our feelings, it is right to do, steadies the pulse, clears the eye and preserves the tranquility of the soul. And there is always something which it is right to do, even in the most desperate circumstances, if it be only to maintain our dignity as human beings, to keep up the drooping spirits of those around us, and to assist our weaker brethren to the last.

—Felix Adler.
Life and Destiny: Or, Thoughts from the Ethical Lectures of Felix Adler.

Though a river flows in full stream, stillness reigns in the neighborhood. Nature thus teaches us that, though our environment is noisy, we can keep our minds serene and unruffled.

—Hung Ying-Ming.
Musings of a Chinese Vegetarian.

Calmness is the rarest quality in human life. It is the poise of a great nature, in harmony with itself and its ideals. It is the moral atmosphere of a life self-centred, self-reliant, and self-controlled.

Calmness comes ever from within. It is the peace and restfulness of the depths of our nature. The fury of storm and of wind agitate only the surface of the sea; they can penetrate only two or three hundred feet,—below that is the calm, unruffled deep. To be ready for the great crises of life we must learn serenity in our daily living. Calmness is the crown of self-control.

—William George Jordan.
The Majesty of Calmness.

The Buddha's teaching, Adapting oneself to circumstances, and our Confucian precept, Doing what is due to one's situation, rich or poor,—these sayings are the life-buoys indispensable for navigating the rough sea of life. Boundless are the paths of human existence; in our journey along them, we are bound to meet with numberless rubs and obstacles. If we long for perfection, we shall be annoyed with a thousand worries. On the contrary, if we are contented with our lot, there is not any position in society but gives us peace of mind.

—Hung Ying-Ming.
Musings of a Chinese Vegetarian.

Chapter 31

On Simplicity, Small Things, the Essentials

A little spring had lost its way amid the grass and fern,
A passing stranger scooped a well, where weary men might turn;
He walled it in, and hung with care a ladle at the brink;
He thought not of the deed he did, but judged that toil might drink.
He passed again, and lo! the well, by summers never dried,
Had cooled ten thousand parching tongues, and saved a life besides.

A dreamer dropped a random thought; 't was old, and yet 't was new;
A simple fancy of the brain, but strong in being true.
It shone upon a genial mind, and lo! its light became
A lamp of life, a beacon ray, a monitory flame.
The thought was small; its issue great; a watch-fire on the hill,
It shed its radiance far adown, and cheers the valley still!

A nameless man, amid the crowd that thronged the daily mart,
Let fall a word of Hope and Love, unstudied, from the heart;
A whisper on the tumult thrown,—a transitory breath,—
It raised a brother from the dust; it saved a soul from death.
O germ! O fount! O word of love! O thought at random cast!
Ye were but little at the first, but mighty at the last.

—Charles Mackay.
"Little at First—But Great at Last." *Voices from the Mountains and from the Crowd.*

In its dreams, man's ambition embraces vast limits, but it is rarely given us to achieve great things, and even then, a quick and sure success always rests on a groundwork of patient preparation. Fidelity in small things is at the base of every great achievement. We too often forget this, and yet no truth needs more to be kept in mind, particularly in the troubled eras of history and in the crises of individual life. In shipwreck a splintered beam, an oar, any scrap of wreckage, saves us. On the tumbling waves of life, when everything seems shattered to fragments, let us not forget that a single one of these poor bits may become our plank of safety. To despise the remnants is demoralization.

—CHARLES WAGNER.
The Simple Life.

We scale the mountain's rugged side, not at one mighty leap,
But step by step and breath by breath we climb the lofty steep.
Each simple duty comes alone our willing strength to try;
One little moment at a time and so the days go by.
With strength to lift and heart to hope, we strive from sun to sun,
A little here, a little there, and all our tasks are done...

—NIXON WATERMAN.
"This Busy World." <i>The Girl Wanted.</i>

Think nought a trifle, though it small appear;
Small sands the mountain, moments make the year,
And trifles life. Your care to trifles give,
Or you may die, before you truly live.

—Edward Young.
Love of Fame, The Universal Passion. In Seven Characteristical Satires.

Simplicity is the elimination of the non-essential in all things. It reduces life to its minimum of real needs; raises it to its maximum of powers. Simplicity means the survival,—not of the fittest, but of the best. In morals it kills the weeds of vice and weakness so that the flowers of virtue and strength may have room to grow. Simplicity cuts off waste and intensifies concentration. It converts flickering torches into searchlights.

Let us seek to cultivate this simplicity in all things in our life. The first step toward simplicity is "simplifying." The beginning of mental or moral progress or reform is always renunciation or sacrifice. It is rejection, surrender or destruction of separate phases of habit or life that have kept us from higher things.

The secret of all true greatness is simplicity. Make simplicity the keynote of your life and you will be great, no matter though your life be humble and your influence seem but little. Simple habits, simple manners, simple needs, simple words, simple faiths,—all are the pure manifestations of a mind and heart of simplicity.

—William George Jordan.
Self-Control, Its Kingship and Majesty.

That is the simple life—direct and immediate contact with things, life with the false wrappings torn away—............

….. to be in direct and personal contact with the sources of your material life; to want no extras, no shields; to find the universal elements enough; to find the air and the water exhilarating; to be refreshed by a morning walk or an evening saunter; to find a quest of wild berries more satisfying than a gift of tropic fruit; to be thrilled by the stars at night; to be elated over a bird's nest, or a wild flower in spring—these are some of the rewards of the simple life.

—JOHN BURROUGHS.
"An Outlook Upon Life." *Leaf and Tendril.*

The less we have to do in life, the higher shall we rise above the world. Have a small circle of friendship, and we shall have less trouble and entanglement in society. Be few in our words, and we shall have fewer mistakes and misunderstandings. Be limited in our thoughts and worries, and we shall have less waste of our energies. Spare the working of our senses, and our nature will be in freer play, as we have less occasion to be annoyed by our surroundings. Those who increase the amount of their work daily, instead of decreasing it, only make fetters and shackles of their lives.

—HUNG YING-MING.
Musings of a Chinese Vegetarian.

The small events of life, taken singly, may seem exceedingly unimportant, like snow that falls silently, flake by flake; yet accumulated, these snow-flakes form the avalanche.

As daylight can be seen through very small holes, so little things will illustrate a person's character. Indeed character consists in little acts, well and honourably performed; daily life being the quarry from which we build it up, and rough-hew the habits which form it.

The little courtesies which form the small change of life, may separately appear of little intrinsic value, but they acquire their importance from repetition and accumulation. They are like the spare minutes, or the groat a day, which proverbially produce such momentous results in the course of a twelvemonth, or in a lifetime.

Who could have imagined that the famous "chalk cliffs of Albion" had been built up by tiny insects—detected only by the help of the microscope—of the same order of creatures that have gemmed the sea with islands of coral! And who that contemplates such extraordinary results, arising from infinitely minute operations, will venture to question the power of little things?

—SAMUEL SMILES.
Self-help; with illustrations of character and conduct.

The movement towards simplicity is after all a movement towards a deeper spirituality which is a movement towards reality. Simplicity is getting to the heart of things, stripping them of their non-essentials and laying hold of the real which is the spiritual.

Simplicity is not trying to be. Simplicity is sincerity, naturalness, manliness, self-government, the subordination of the lower to the higher, or of the higher to the highest—in one word, sacrifice; or if a fuller phrase be asked, finding the divine plan and fulfilling it.

Thus does simplicity in its highest phase become the spiritualization of life!

—MALCOLM JAMES MCLEOD.
"Simplicity and Spirituality." *The Culture of Simplicity.*

.... 'There's nothing great
Nor small', has said a poet of our day,
(Whose voice will ring beyond the curfew of eve
And not be thrown out by the matin's bell)
And truly, I reiterate, ... nothing's small!
No lily-muffled hum of a summer-bee,
But finds some coupling with the spinning stars;
No pebble at your foot, but proves a sphere;
No chaffinch, but implies the cherubim...

—ELIZABETH BARRETT BROWNING.
Aurora Leigh.

Time is so precious that its smallest particles are valuable, and for him that knows how to utilize them the hours acquire a singular capacity—in one of them years may be condensed, even centuries.

The sculptor finds a bit of marble, and carves a masterpiece. On a scrap of waste-paper the poet in an idle hour writes an immortal song. Collect the stones that lie helter-skelter in this gorge, and you might build a cathedral. Is not the earth made from a fragment of the sun, and man from a breath of the Infinite?

—Charles Wagner.
The Better Way.

A spark is a molecule of matter, yet may it kindle the world:
Vast is the mighty ocean, but drops have made it vast.
Despise not thou a small thing, either for evil or for good;
For a look may work thy ruin, or a word create thy wealth:
The walking this way or that, the casual stopping or hastening,
Hath saved life, and destroyed it, hath cast down and built up fortunes.
Commit thy trifles unto God, for to Him is nothing trivial;
And it is but the littleness of man that seeth no greatness in a trifle.
All things are infinite in parts, and the moral is as the material,
Neither is anything vast, but it is compacted of atoms.
Thou art wise, and shalt find comfort, if thou study thy pleasure in trifles,
For slender joys, often repeated, fall as sunshine on the heart:

—Martin Farquhar Tupper.
"Of Trifles." *Proverbial Philosophy: A Book of Thoughts and Arguments.*

Chapter 32

On Patience, Waiting, Forbearance

It is in length of patience, and endurance, and forbearance, that so much of what is good in mankind and womankind is shown.

—Arthur Helps.
Realmah.

To be resign'd when ills betide,
Patient when favours are denied,
And pleas'd with favours given;
Dear Chloe, this is wisdoms part,
This is that incense of the heart,
Whose fragrance smells to Heaven.

—Nathaniel Cotton.
"The Fire-Side." *The Works of the British Poets: With Prefaces, Biographical and Critical, Volume 11.*

The first great rule of life, according to Epictetus, is to put up with things: he makes that the moiety of wisdom. To put up with all the varieties of folly would need much patience. We often have to put up with most from those on whom we most depend: a useful lesson in self-control.

Out of patience comes forth peace, the priceless boon which is the happiness of the world.

—BALTASAR GRACIÁN.
The Art of Worldly Wisdom.

Beareth all things, believeth all things, hopeth all things, endureth all things.

—1 CORINTHIANS 13:7. *KJV.*

Thou oughtest therefore to call to mind the more grievous sufferings of others that thou mightest bear thy lesser ones more easily, and if they seem not to thee little, see that it is not thy impatience which is the cause of this. But whether they be little or whether they be great, study to bear them all with patience.

…and if tribulation hath touched thee, yet let it not cast thee down nor entangle thee long. At the least, bear patiently, if thou canst not joyfully.

—THOMAS À KEMPIS.
"Third Book." *The Imitation of Christ.*

Better is the end of a thing than the beginning thereof: and the patient in spirit is better than the proud in spirit.

—ECCLESIASTES 7:8. *KJV.*

Progress, however, of the best kind, is comparatively slow. Great results cannot be achieved at once; and we must be satisfied to advance in life as we walk, step by step. De Maistre says that "to know how to wait is the great secret of success." We must sow before we can reap, and often have to wait long, content meanwhile to look patiently forward in hope; the fruit best worth waiting for often ripening the slowest. But "time and patience," says the Eastern proverb, "change the mulberry leaf to satin."

—Samuel Smiles.
Self-help; with illustrations of character and conduct.

Leave this military hurry and adopt the pace of Nature. Her secret is patience.

—Ralph Waldo Emerson.
"Education." *Education: An Essay and Other Selections.*

Who bides his time, and day by day
Faces defeat full patiently,
And lifts a mirthful roundelay,
However poor his fortunes be,
He will not fail in any qualm
Of poverty - the paltry dime
It will grow golden in his palm,
Who bides his time.

Who bides his time - he tastes the sweet
Of honey in the saltest tear;
And though he fares with slowest feet,

Joy runs to meet him, drawing near;
The birds are heralds of his cause;
And like a never-ending rhyme,
The roadsides bloom in his applause,
Who bides his time.

—James Whitcomb Riley.
"Who Bides His Time."

And not only so, but we glory in tribulations also: knowing that tribulation worketh patience;
And patience, experience; and experience, hope:

—Romans 5:3-4. *KJV.*

Our real blessings often appear to us in the shape of pains, losses and disappointments; but let us have patience and we soon shall see them in their proper figures.

—Joseph Addison.
The Guardian. No. 117. The Works of the Right Honourable Joseph Addison, Volume 4.

Forbearance and self-control smooth the road of life, and open many ways which would otherwise remain closed.

—Samuel Smiles.
"Chapter VII. Self-Control." *Character.*

I only design to exhibit what many are so apt to overlook or forget, the sublime efficacy of those virtues which belong to the receiving, suffering, patient side of character. They are such as meekness, gentleness, forbearance, forgiveness, the endurance of wrong without anger and resentment, contentment, quietness, peace, and unambitious love. These all belong to the more passive side of character and are included, or may be, in the general and comprehensive term patience.

—Horace Bushnell.
"The Efficiency of the Passive Virtues."
Sermons for the New Life.

Let us as individuals banish the word "Hurry" from our lives. Let us care for nothing so much that we would pay honor and self-respect as the price of hurrying it. Let us cultivate calmness, restfulness, poise, sweetness,—doing our best, bearing all things as bravely as we can; living our life undisturbed by the prosperity of the wicked or the malice of the envious. Let us not be impatient, chafing at delay, fretting over failure, wearying over results, and weakening under opposition. Let us ever turn our face toward the future with confidence and trust, with the calmness of a life in harmony with itself, true to its ideals, and slowly and constantly progressing toward their realization.

—William George Jordan.
The Majesty of Calmness.

….. let us lay aside every weight, and the sin which doth so easily beset us, and let us run with patience the race that is set before us.

—HEBREWS 12:1 *KJV*.

We must be satisfied to work with a purpose, and wait the results with patience. All progress, of the best kind, is slow; but to him who works faithfully and zealously the reward will, doubtless, be vouchsafed in good time.

—SAMUEL SMILES.
Self-help; with illustrations of character and conduct.

…it is a blessed thing to be patient; that a quietness of spirit hath a certain reward….

—JEREMY TAYLOR.
The Beauties of Jeremy Taylor, D.D.
Selected from His Works.

Chapter 33

ON HUMILITY, HUMBLENESS

The great Tao flows unobstructed in every direction.
All things rely on it to conceive and be born,
and it does not deny even the smallest of creation.
When it has accomplished great wonders,
it does not claim them for itself.
It nourishes infinite worlds,
yet it doesn't seek to master the smallest creature.
Since it is without wants and desires,
it can be considered humble.
All of creation seeks it for refuge
yet it does not seek to master or control.

—Lao-Tzu.
Tao Te Ching.

Let us be humble if we have great possessions, for that proves that we are great debtors: all that a man has he owes to someone, and are we sure of being able to pay our debts?

Let us be humble if we sit in high places and hold the fate of others in our hands; for no clear-sighted man can fail to be sensible of unfitness for so grave a role.

Let us be humble if we have much knowledge, for it only serves to better show the vastness of the unknown, and to compare the little we have discovered for ourselves with the amplitude of that which we owe to the pains of others.

And, above all, let us be humble if we are virtuous, since no one should be more sensible of his defects than he whose conscience is illumined.

—CHARLES WAGNER.
The Simple Life.

Knowledge is proud that he has learned so much,
Wisdom is humble that he knows no more.

—WILLIAM COWPER.
"The Task." *The Task and Other Poems.*

We need something of the virility of stoicism to grapple with the difficulties of life; we need to cultivate a large patience; an humble spirit that teaches us to be prepared for every loss, and to welcome every joy as an unlooked-for gain.

—FELIX ADLER.
Life and Destiny: Or, Thoughts from the Ethical Lectures of Felix Adler.

The great view the small as their source,
and the high takes the low as their foundation.
Their greatest asset becomes their humility.
They speak of themselves as orphans and widows,
thus they truly seek humility.
Do not shine like the precious gem,
but be as dull as a common stone.

—LAO-TZU.
Tao Te Ching.

But the crowning grace of all is Humility, in the sense in which it implies and presupposes dignity. Dignity is based upon the consciousness of a divine element in human nature, of an infinite aim, a boundless destiny. Humbleness is due to a sense of the incalculable distance which still separates us from the goal. These two, inseparably combined, are the invariable accompaniment of moral greatness wherever met with.

—FELIX ADLER.
Life and Destiny: Or, Thoughts from the Ethical Lectures of Felix Adler.

And before honor is humility.

—PROVERBS 15:33. *KJV.*

For all the world, all that we are, and all that we have, our bodies and our souls, our actions and our sufferings, our conditions at home, our accidents abroad, our many sins, and our seldom virtues, are as so many arguments to make our souls dwell low in the deep valleys of humility.

—Jeremy Taylor.
The Rules and Exercises of Holy Living.

Humility is the softening shadow before the stature of Excellence,
And lieth lowly on the ground, beloved and lovely as the violet:
Humility is the fair-haired maid, that calleth Worth her brother,
The gentle silent nurse, that fostereth infant virtues:
Humility bringeth no excuse; she is welcome to God and to man:
Her countenance is needful unto all, who would prosper in either world.

—Martin Farquhar Tupper.
"Of Humility." *Proverbial Philosophy: A Book of Thoughts and Arguments.*

The bird that soars on highest wing,
Builds on the ground her lowly nest;
And she that doth most sweetly sing,
Sings in the shade, where all things rest:
In lark and nightingale we see
What honor hath humility.

—James Montgomery.
"Humility." *A Poet's Portfolio; or, Minor Poems: in Three Books.*

Pitch thy behaviour low, thy projects high;
So shalt thou humble and magnanimous be.

—GEORGE HERBERT.
"The Church Porch."

Patience is the guardian of faith, the preserver of peace, the cherisher of love, the teacher of humility.

—BISHOP GEORGE HORNE.
Prose Quotations from Socrates to Macaulay.

Humility, that low, sweet root,
From which all heavenly virtues shoot.

—THOMAS MOORE.
The Loves of the Angels: A Poem.

"Do you wish to be great?" asks St. Augustine. "Then begin by being little. Do you desire to construct a vast and lofty fabric? Think first about the foundations of humility. The higher your structure is to be, the deeper must be its foundation. Modest humility is beauty's crown."

—SAMUEL SMILES.
Duty: With Illustrations of Courage, Patience and Endurance.

Humility is like a tree, whose root, when it sets deepest in the earth, rises higher, and spreads fairer, and stands surer, and lasts longer; every step of its descent is like a rib of iron....

—JEREMY TAYLOR.
The Whole Works of the Right Rev. Jeremy Taylor.

A flower more sacred than far-seen success
Perfumes my solitary path; I find
Sweet compensation in my humbleness,
And reap the harvest of a tranquil mind.

—JOHN TOWNSEND TROWBRIDGE.
"Twoscore and Ten."

Chapter 34

On Kindness, Benevolence, Compassion, Mercy

The quality of mercy is not strained,
It droppeth as the gentle rain from heaven
Upon the place beneath. It is twice blest,
It blesseth him that gives and him that takes.
'Tis mightiest in the mightiest, it becomes
The thronèd monarch better than his crown.
His sceptre shows the force of temporal power,
The attribute to awe and majesty,
Wherein doth sit the dread and fear of kings;
But mercy is above this sceptred sway,
It is enthronèd in the hearts of kings,
It is an attribute to God himself,
And earthly power doth then show likest God's
When mercy seasons justice.

—William Shakespeare.
"Act IV, Scene 1". *The Merchant of Venice.*

Love the whole world as if it were your self;
then you will truly care for all things.

—Lao-Tzu.
Tao Te Ching.

He sees the poor Hebrew: he stops on the way.
—By the side of the wretched 't is better to pray,
Than to visit the holiest temple that stands
In the thrice blessed places of Palestine's lands.
The oil that was meant for Mount Gerizim's ground,
Would better be poured on the sufferer's wound;
For no incense more sweetly, more purely can rise
From the altars of earth to the throne of the skies,
No libation more rich can be offered below,
Than that which is tendered to anguish and woe.

> —John G. C. Brainard.
> "The Good Samaritan." *The Poems of John G. C. Brainard: a new and authentic collection, with an original memoir of his life.*

We are to relieve the distressed; to put the wanderer into his way; and to divide our bread with the hungry: which is but the doing of good to ourselves; for we are only several members of one great body. Nay, we are all of a consanguinity; formed of the same materials, and designed to the same end; this obliges us to a mutual tenderness and converse; and the other, to live with a regard to equity and justice.

> —Lucius Annaeus Seneca.
> "Of a Happy Life."

Large bounties to bestow we wish in vain;
But all may shun the guilt of giving pain.
To bless Mankind with tides of flowing wealth,
With pow'r to grace them, or to crown with health,

Our little lot denies; but Heav'n decrees
To all, the gift of minist'ring to ease.
The gentle offices of patient love,
Beyond all flatt'ry, and all price above;
The mild forbearance at another's fault,
The taunting word suppress'd as soon as thought;
On these Heav'n bade the bliss of life depend,
And crush'd ill fortune when he made a Friend.

A Solitary blessing few can find,
Our joys with those we love are intertwin'd;
And he, whose helpful tenderness removes
Th' obstructing thorn which wounds the breast he loves,
Smooths not another's rugged path alone,
But scatters roses to adorn his own.

—Hannah More.
"Sensibility: An Epistle to the Honourable Mrs. Boscawen." *Sacred Dramas.*

Who are the Blest?
They who have kept their sympathies awake,
And scattered good for more than custom's sake;
Steadfast and tender in the hour of need,
Gentle in thought, benevolent in deed;
Whose looks have power to make dissension cease—
Whose smiles are pleasant, and whose words are peace;—
They who have lived as harmless as the dove,
Teachers of truth, and ministers of love,—
Love for all moral power, all mental grace,
Love for the humblest of the human race,—
Love for that tranquil joy which virtue brings,—

Love for the Giver of all goodly things.

—JOHN CRITCHLEY PRINCE.
"Who Are the Free!" *Hours with the Muses.*

Self-love thus pushed to social, to divine,
Gives thee to make thy neighbour's blessing thine.
Is this too little for the boundless heart?
Extend it, let thy enemies have part:
Grasp the whole worlds of reason, life, and sense,
In one close system of benevolence:
Happier as kinder, in whate'er degree,
And height of bliss but height of charity.

—ALEXANDER POPE.
"Epistle IV." *An Essay on Man. Moral Essays and Satires.*

When the nations, too, cease to be savage and selfish, and become altruistic, then the new birth of humanity will actually have occurred. As an artist and a creator of beautiful forms, man has also had his day; he loved the beautiful, the artistic, or the ornamental long before he loved the true and the just. He was proud before he was kind; he was chivalrous before he was decent; he was tattooed before he was washed; he was painted before he was clothed; he built temples before he built a home; he sacrificed to his gods before he helped his neighbor; he was heroic before he was self-denying; he was devout before he was charitable. We are losing the savage virtues and vanities and growing in the grace of all the humanities, and this process will doubtless go on, with many interruptions and setbacks of course, till the kingdom of love is at last fairly established upon the earth.

—JOHN BURROUGHS.
"The Worm Striving to Be Man." *Time and Change.*

No gift so cheap as love is cheap,
Yet none so rich may be
As they who on their altars keep
The lamp of sympathy.

A forest dark, bewildering,
This life we wander through;
Praise God for those who work and sing,
For both we have to do—
Our greater mission not to win
The thing we most desire,
But more to keep, through care and sin,
Our hearts with love afire.

For there are others on the road,
The dark and misty trail,
And we who bear the lighter load
Must help the ones who fail;
And, helping on the weary soul
Who stumbles by alone,
Thus we, in striving for his goal,
Shall come upon our own.

—DOUGLAS MALLOCH.
"Sympathy." *In Forest Land.*

If you sit down at set of sun
And count the acts that you have done,
And, counting, find
One self-denying deed, one word
That eased the heart of him who heard,
One glance most kind
That fell like sunshine where it went—
Then you may count that day well spent.

But if, through all the livelong day,
You've cheered no heart, by yea or nay—
If, through it all
You've nothing done that you can trace
That brought the sunshine to one face—
No act most small
That helped some soul and nothing cost—
Then count that day as worse than lost.

—GEORGE ELIOT. (MARY ANNE EVANS).
"Count That Day Lost."

When we count our gold at the end of the day,
And have filtered the dross that has cumbered the way,
Oh, what were the hold of our treasury then
Save the love we have shown to the children of men?

—GEORGIA DOUGLAS JOHNSON.
"Service." *Bronze: A Book of Verse.*

A sense of an earnest Will
To help the lowly-living,—

And a terrible heart-thrill,
If you have no power of giving;
An arm of aid to the weak,
A friendly hand to the friendless,
Kind words, so short to speak,
But whose echo is endless:
The world is wide,—these things are small,
They may be nothing, but they are All.

—Richard Monckton Milnes.
"Moments." *Poems of Many Years.*

For oft from the darkness of hearts and lives
Come songs that brim with joy and light,
As out of the gloom of the cypress grove
The mocking-bird sings at night.

So I sang a lay for a brother's ear
In a strain to soothe his bleeding heart,
And he smiled at the sound of my voice and lyre,
Though mine was a feeble art.

But at his smile I smiled in turn,
And into my soul there came a ray:
In trying to soothe another's woes
Mine own had passed away.

—Paul Laurence Dunbar.
"The Lesson." *Lyrics of Lowly Life.*

Chapter 35

On Successful Living, Living With Purpose

They err who measure life by years,
With false or thoughtless tongue;
Some hearts grow old before their time;
Others are always young.

'Tis not the number of the lines
On life's fast filling page, -
'Tis not the pulse's added throbs,
Which constitute their age.

Some souls are serfs among the free,
While others nobly thrive;
They stand just where their fathers stood;
Dead, even while they live!

Others, all spirit, heart, and sense;
Theirs the mysterious power
To live in thrills of joy or woe,
A twelvemonth in an hour!

Seize, them the minutes as they pass,
The woof of life is thought!
Warm up the colours; let them glow
With fire and fancy frought.

Live to some purpose; make thy life
A gift of use to thee:
A joy, a good, a golden hope,
A heavenly argosy!

—Bryan Waller Procter.
"The Gauge of Life."

At no epoch have the exterior conditions which man has made for himself by his industry or his knowledge, been able to exempt him from care for the state of his inner life. The face of the world alters around us, its intellectual and material factors vary; and no one can arrest these changes, whose suddenness is sometimes not short of perilous. But the important thing is that at the center of shifting circumstance man should remain man, live his life, make toward his goal. And whatever be his road, to make toward his goal, the traveler must not lose himself in crossways, nor hamper his movements with useless burdens. Let him heed well his direction and forces, and keep good faith; and that he may the better devote himself to the essential—which is to progress—at whatever sacrifice, let him simplify his baggage.

—Charles Wagner.
The Simple Life.

Until thought is linked with purpose there is no intelligent accomplishment.

To put away aimlessness and weakness, and to begin to think

with purpose, is to enter the ranks of those strong ones who only recognize failure as one of the pathways to attainment; who make all conditions serve them, and who think strongly, attempt fearlessly, and accomplish masterfully.

Thought allied fearlessly to purpose becomes creative force.

—JAMES ALLEN.
As a Man Thinketh.

To feed my soul with beauty till I die;
To give my hands a pleasant task to do;
To keep my heart forever filled anew
With dreams and wonders which the days supply;
To love all conscious living, and thereby
Respect the brute who renders up its due,
And know the world as planned is good and true—
And thus—because there chanced to be an I.

—WILLIAM STANLEY BRAITHWAITE.
"This is My Life." *The House of Falling Leaves with Other Poems.*

And yet, for those who know
Themselves, who wisely take
Their way through life, and bow
To what they cannot break,
Why should I say that life need yield but moderate bliss?

Shall we, with temper spoil'd,
Health sapp'd by living ill,
And judgment all embroil'd

By sadness and self-will,
Shall we judge what for man is not true bliss or is?

Is it so small a thing
To have enjoy'd the sun,
To have lived light in the spring,
To have loved, to have thought, to have done;
To have advanced true friends, and beat down baffling foes—

That we must feign a bliss
Of doubtful future date,
And, while we dream on this,
Lose all our present state,
And relegate to worlds yet distant our repose?

—MATTHEW ARNOLD.
"Empedocles on Etna." *Empedocles on Etna, and Other Poems.*

Keep your heart free from hate, your mind from worry. Live simply; expect little; give much; sing often; pray always. Fill your life with love. Scatter sunshine. Forget self. Think of others. Do as you would be done by—these are the tried links in contentment's golden chain.

—MALCOLM JAMES MCLEOD.
"Simplicity and Happiness." *The Culture of Simplicity.*

The secret of culture is to learn, that a few great points steadily reappear, alike in the poverty of the obscurest farm, and in the miscellany of metropolitan life, and that these few are alone to be regarded,—the escape from all false ties; courage to be what we are; and love of what is simple and beautiful; independence, and cheerful relation, these are the essentials,—these, and the wish to serve,—to add somewhat to the well-being of men.

—RALPH WALDO EMERSON.
"Considerations by the Way." *The Conduct of Life.*

What is noble?—to inherit
Wealth, estate, and proud degree?—
There must be some other merit
Higher yet than these for me!—
Something greater far must enter
Into life's majestic span,
Fitted to create and centre
True nobility in man.

What is noble?—'tis the finer
Portion of our mind and heart,
Linked to something still diviner
Than mere language can impart;
Ever prompting—ever seeing
Some improvement yet to plan;
To uplight our fellow being,
And, like man, to feel for Man!

What is noble?—that which places
Truth in its enfranchised will,
Leaving steps—like angel traces,
That mankind may follow still!
E'en though scorn's ungrateful glances
Prove him poorest of his clan,

He's the Noble—who advances
Freedom, and the Cause of Man!

—CHARLES SWAIN.
"What is Noble?". *Selections from Charles Swain.*

Cherish your visions. Cherish your ideals. Cherish the music that stirs in your heart, the beauty that forms in your mind, the loveliness that drapes your purest thoughts, for out of them will grow all delightful conditions, all heavenly environment; of these, if you but remain true to them, your world will at last be built.

—JAMES ALLEN.
As a Man Thinketh.

REFERENCES

Addison, Joseph. *The Guardian. No. 117. The Works of the Right Honourable Joseph Addison, Volume IV*. Bell & Daldy, 1866.

—-. *The Works of the Right Honourable Joseph Addison, Volume IV*. Collected by Mr. Tickell. Vernor and Hood, et al,1804.

Adler, Felix. *Life and Destiny: Or, Thoughts from the Ethical Lectures of Felix Adler*. McClure, Phillips & Company, 1903.

Alcott, Louisa May. "My Kingdom."

Allen, James. *Above Life's Turmoil.*

—-. *As a Man Thinketh.*

—-. *The Way of Peace.*

Amiel, Henri-Frédéric. *Amiel's Journal: The Journal Intime of Henri-Frédéric Amiel*. Translated, With an Introduction and Notes by Mrs. Humphrey Ward. MacMillan and Company, 1894, 1915.

Arnold, Edwin. *The Light of Asia: Or, The Great Renunciation.*

Arnold, Matthew. "Empedocles on Etna." *Empedocles on Etna, and Other Poems*. B. Fellowes, 1852.

—-. "Morality." *Poetical Works of Matthew Arnold.*

Aurelius, Marcus. *The Meditations of Marcus Aurelius.* Translated by George Long.

Bailey, Philip James. "Proem." *Festus: A Poem.* James Miller, 1872.

—-. "Scene-A Village Feast-Evening." *Festus. A Poem.* B. B. Mussey, 1853.

Bates, David. "Speak Gently." *The Eolian.* Lindsay & Blakiston, 1849.

—-. "The World of Mind."

Beaumont, Joseph. "The House of the Mind." *A Manual of Spiritual Fortification.* Made and annotated by Louise Collier Willcox. Harper & Brothers Publishers, 1910.

Benjamin, Park. "Press On." *The Golden Treasury of Poetry and Prose.* Edited by Francis Fisher Browne. N.D. Thompson and Company, 1883.

Bennoch, Francis. "My Books." *The Storm, and Other Poems.* William Smith, William Tait, J.B. Sinclair, 1841.

Besant, Annie. "Problems of Ethics". *Some Problems of Life.* Theosophical Publishing Society, 1900.

The Bhagavad-Gita (from the *Mahabharata).* Translated from the Sanskrit Text by Sir Edwin Arnold. Truslove, Hanson & Comba, Ltd., 1900.

Boethius. "Book I. Song VI." *The Consolation of Philosophy of Boethius.* Translated into English Prose and Verse by H. R. James. Elliot Stock,1897.

—-. "Book III. Song II."

—-. "Book III. Song XI."

—-. "Book IV. Song VI."

Bolton, Sarah Knowles. "The Inevitable." *An American Anthology, 1787-1900*. Edited by Edmund Clarence Stedman. Houghton, Mifflin and Company, 1900.

Brainard, John G. C. "The Good Samaritan." *The Poems of John G. C. Brainard: a new and authentic collection, with an original memoir of his life*. S. Andrus and Son, 1847.

Braithwaite, William Stanley. "The Eternal Self (to Vere Goldthwaite)." *The House of Falling Leaves with Other Poems*. John. W. Luce and Company, 1908.

—-. "This is My Life."

—-. "Thanksgiving." *Lyrics of Life and Love*. Herbert B. Turner and Company, 1904.

Browning, Elizabeth Barrett. "An Essay on Mind." *An Essay on Mind, with Other Poems*. (Published anonymously). James Duncan, 1826.

—-. *Aurora Leigh*. Chapman and Hall, 1857.

Burroughs, John. "The Natural Providence." *Accepting the Universe. Essays in Naturalism*. Houghton Mifflin Company, 1920.

—-. "The Art of Seeing Things." *Leaf and Tendril*. Houghton, Mifflin and Company, 1908.

—-. "An Outlook Upon Life."

—-. "The Phantoms Behind Us." *Time and Change*. Houghton Mifflin Company, 1912.

—-. "The Worm Striving to Be Man."

Bushnell, Horace. "The Efficiency of the Passive Virtues." *Sermons for the New Life*. Charles Scribner, 1858.

Butler, Frances Anne (late Fanny Kemble). "Lines, Addressed to the Young Gentlemen leaving the Academy at Lennox, Massachusetts." *Poems*. Henry Washbourne, 1844.

Carter, Elizabeth. "Ode to Wisdom."

Carlyle, Thomas. "Characteristics." *The Edinburgh Review*. Vol. LIV. December, 1831.

—-. "The Hero as Divinity." *On Heroes, Hero-worship and the Heroic in History*.

> —-. "The Hero as Man of Letters."

> —-. "The Hero as Poet."

—-. "Chapter 12. Reward." *Past and Present*.

—-. "Book I. Chapter XI. Prospective." *Sartor Resartus*.

—-. "The Opera." *The Works of Thomas Carlyle: Critical and Miscellaneous Essays. In Five Volumes*. Chapman and Hall, 1899.

—-. "Signs of the Times."

Cary, Phoebe. "Aspirations."

—-. "Now." *The Poetical Works of Alice and Phoebe Cary*. Houghton, Mifflin and Company, Riverside Press, 1884.

Chalmers, Thomas. "The Supremacy of Conscience." *On Natural Theology. Volume 1*. Robert Carter & Brothers, 1857.

Charles, Elizabeth Rundle. "The Cruse That Faileth Not." *The Women of the Gospels: The Three Wakings, and Other Poems*. M.W. Dodd, 1867.

Chuang Tzu. *Chuang Tzu Mystic, Moralist, and Social Reformer*. Translated from the Chinese by Herbert A. Giles. Bernard Quaritch, 1889.

Cicero, Marcus Tullius. *Cicero: de Officiis*. With an English Translation by Walter Miller. William Heinemann, LTD., 1913.

Clemmer, Mary. "Silence." *Poems of Life and Nature*. James R. Osgood and Company, 1883.

Cody, Rosalie May. "Thanksgiving." *In Flight*. Duffield and Company, 1916.

Coleridge, Samuel Taylor. "Inscription for a Time-Piece." *The Poems of Samuel Taylor Coleridge*. Edited by Derwent and Sara Coleridge. Edward, Moxon, 1856.

Colton, Charles Caleb. *Lacon: Or, Many Things in Few Words; Addressed to Those who Think*. Longman, Orme, Brown, Green, & Longmans, 1837.

Cotton, Nathaniel. "The Fire-Side." *The Works of the British Poets: With Prefaces, Biographical and Critical, Volume 11*. By Robert Anderson. John & Arthur Arch, 1795.

Cousins, James H. "The Quest." *The Quest*. Maunsel and Co., Ltd, 1906.

Cowper, William. "The Task." *The Task and Other Poems*. Cassell and Company, Limited, 1899.

Cox, Kenyon. "The Gospel of Art." *Hoyt's New Cyclopedia of Practical Quotations*. Funk & Wagnalls Company, 1922.

De Sales (St), Francis. *A Selection from the Spiritual Letters of s. Francis de Sales*. Translated by Henrietta Louisa Lear. Rivingtons, 1880.

De Vere, Aubrey. "Sorrow."

Dewey, Orville. *Autobiography and Letters of Orville Dewey, D.D.* Edited by his Daughter Mary E. Dewey. Roberts Brothers, 1883.

The Dhammapada. Translated from the Pali by F. Max Muller. *Volume X of The Sacred Books of the East.* Oxford, the Clarendon Press, 1881.

Dickinson, Emily. "The Book." *Poems by Emily Dickinson. 3d series.* Edited by Mabel Loomis Todd. Roberts Brothers, 1896.

Doudney, Sarah. "The Lesson of the Water-Mill." *The Golden Treasury of Poetry and Prose.* Edited by Francis Fisher Browne. N.D. Thompson and Company, 1883.

Dryden, John. *Palemon and Arcite; or the Knight's Tale from Chaucer, Book III.*

Dunbar, Paul Laurence. "Conscience and Remorse." *Lyrics of Lowly Life.* Dodd, Mead and Co., 1896.

—-. "The Lesson."

—-. "The Mystery."

Eastman, Charles Alexander (Ohiyesa.) "Foreword." *The Soul of the Indian: An Interpretation.* Houghton Mifflin Company, 1911.

—-. "The Great Mystery."

Eliot, George. (Mary Anne Evans). "Count That Day Lost."

Ellis, Sarah Stickney (Mrs. Ellis). "Chapter XXXV." *Hearts and Homes; or Social Distinction. A Story.* D. Appleton and Company, 1857.

Emerson, Ralph Waldo. "Considerations by the Way." *The Conduct of Life.*

—-. "Fate."

—-. *The Divinity School Address.*

—-. "Education." *Education: An Essay and Other Selections.* Houghton Mifflin Company, 1909.

—-. *Essays, First Series.*

    —-. "Compensation."

    —-. "The Over-Soul."

    —-. "Self-Reliance."

—-. "Immortality." *Letters and Social Aims. Volume 8.* Macmillan and Company, 1883.

—-. "Poetry and Imagination."

—-. "Nature." *Essays, Second Series.*

Fénelon, Francois de Salignac de La Mothe. *A Demonstration of the Existence and Attributes of God.* William Gillmor, 1811.

Fosdick, Harry Emerson. *Twelve Tests of Character.* Association Press, 1923.

Fuller, Arthur Buckminster. "Preface." *Life Without and Life Within, Or, Reviews, Narratives, Essays, and Poems* by Margaret Fuller (Margaret Fuller Ossoli). Brown, Taggard and Chase, 1859.

Fullerton, Lady Georgiana. *Grantley Manor: A Tale.* D. Appleton & Company, 1849.

Gay, John. "The Shepherd and the Philosopher." *The Poetical Works of John Gay. With a life of the author by Dr. Johnson*. Little, Brown, and Company, 1854.

Gibran, Kahlil. *The Prophet*. Alfred A Knopf, 1923.

Goethe, Johann Wolfgang von. "Prelude in the Theatre." *Faust: A Tragedy, translated from the German of Goethe*. Translated with notes by Charles T. Brooks. Ticknor and Fields, 1856.

—-. "#196." *Musical Mosaics: A Collection of Six Hundred Selections from Musical Literature, Ancient and Modern*. Compiled by Willey Francis Gates. T. Presser, 1889.

Goldsmith, Oliver. "On Justice and Generosity. *The Miscellaneous Works of Oliver Goldsmith, M.B.* Published by Peter Brown, 1837.

Gracián, Baltasar. *The Art of Worldly Wisdom*. Translated by Joseph Jacobs. Macmillan and Company, 1892.

Grindon, Leo Hartley. "Chapter XVIII. Life Realized by Activity.—Action the Law of Happiness." *Life: Its Nature, Varieties, and Phenomena*. F. Pitman, 1875.

Guest, Edgar Albert. "Gratitude." *A Heap o' Livin'*. The Reilly and Lee Company, 1916.

—-. "A Toast To Happiness."

Hall, Joseph. *Christian Moderation. (The Works of the Right Reverend Joseph Hall*. University Press, 1863.)

Hartmann, Sadakichi. *My Rubaiyat*. Mangan Printing Co., 1913.

Hathaway, Benjamin. "Work." *Art-life And Other Poems*. H. H. Carter & Company, 1877.

Helps, Arthur. *Realmah*. Roberts Brothers, 1869.

Herbert, George. "The Church Porch." *Lyra Sacra. A Book of Religious Verse*. Selected by H. C. Beeching. Methuen & Co., 1903.

Herrick, Robert. "Happiness." *The Hesperides & Noble Numbers*. Edited by Alfred Pollard. Lawrence & Bullen, Ltd., 1898.

Herschel, John. *Address on the opening of the Eton Library*, 1833.

Hill, Leslie Pinckney. "Nil Desperandum." *The Wings of Oppression*. The Stratford Company, 1921.

Higginson, Thomas Wentworth. *The Sympathy of Religions*. An Address Delivered at Horticultural Hall, Boston, February 6, 1870.

Horne, Bishop George. *Prose Quotations from Socrates to Macaulay*. Compiled by S. Austin Allibone. J. B. Lippincott & Co., 1880.

Horton, George Moses. "The Swan - Vain Pleasures." *The Poetical Works of George M. Horton, The Colored Bard of North Carolina*, 1845.

Hume, David. "Essay 16: The Stoic." *Essays Moral, Political, and Literary, Volume 1*. Edited by Thomas Hill Green, Thomas Hodge Grose. Longmans, Green, and Company, 1875.

Hung Ying-Ming. *Musings of a Chinese Vegetarian*. Translated by Yaichiro Isobe. Yuhodo, Kanda. 1926.

Ingersoll, Robert Green. "Nature." *The Philosophy of Ingersoll*. Edited and arranged by Vere Goldthwaite. Paul Elder and Company, 1906.

Irving, Washington. "The Angler." *The Sketch Book of Geoffrey Crayon, Gent.* G. P. Putnam, 1864.

Jefferies, Richard. *The Pageant of Summer.* Thomas B. Mosher, 1898.

Johnson, Georgia Douglas. "Service." *Bronze: A Book of Verse.* B.J. Brimmer Company, 1922.

—-. "Why."

Johnson, Samuel. *The Vanity of Human Wishes: The Tenth Satire of Juvenal, Imitated by Samuel Johnson.* R. Dodsley, 1749.

Jordan, William George. *The Majesty of Calmness.* Oliphant Anderson & Ferrier, 1902.

—-. *Self-Control, Its Kingship and Majesty.* Fleming H. Revell Company, 1899 and 1905.

Joubert, Joseph. *Pensées of Joubert.* Selected and translated by Henry Attwell. George Allen, 1896.

Judson, L. Carroll. "Prudence." *The Moral Probe or One Hundred and Two Essays on the Nature of Men and Things.* L.C. Judson, 1849.

Kabir. *Songs of Kabir.* Translated by Rabindranath Tagore. The Macmillan Company, 1915.

Kempis, Thomas à. *The Imitation of Christ.* Translated by William Benham.

Kiser, Samuel Ellsworth. "The Fighter."

Langford, John Alfred. "Preliminary Essay." *The Praise of Books, As Said and Sung by English Authors.* Selected by John Alfred Langford. Cassell, Petter, Galpin & Company, 1880.

Lao-Tzu. *Tao Te Ching* by Lao-Tzu. Complete online text, a translation for the public domain by J. H. McDonald, 1996.

Lazarus, Emma. "Work." *The Poems of Emma Lazarus. Narrative, Lyric, and Dramatic*. Houghton, Mifflin and Company, 1889.

Longfellow, Henry Wadsworth. "Book II. Chapter VI. Glimpses into Cloud-land." *Hyperion: A Romance*. John B. Alden, 1885.

—-. *Kavanagh, A Tale*. George Slater, 1849.

—-. *Keramos and Other Poems*. Houghton, Osgood, and Company 1878.

—-. "Keramos."

—-. "The Three Silences of Molinos. To John Greenleaf Whittier."

Lubbock, John. "The Happiness of Duty." *The Pleasures of Life: Part I and Part II*. Macmillan and Co., 1891.

—-. "Music."

Lynch, Anne C. "Thoughts in a Library." *The Female Poets of America*. By Rufus Wilmot Griswold. Henry C. Baird, 1853.

MacCall, William. "Duty."

MacClintock, William Darnall. "Introductory Essay. Young People and the Poets." *The World's Best Poetry*. Edited by Bliss Carman, et al. John D. Morris & Co., 1904.

Mackay, Charles. "Daily Work." *Voices from the Mountains and from the Crowd*. Ticknor, Reed, Fields, 1853.

—-. "Little at First—But Great at Last."

—-. "Serenity."

Malloch, Douglas. "Sympathy." *In Forest Land*. American Lumberman, 1910.

Markham, Edwin. "One Life, One Law." *The Man with the Hoe, and Other Poems*. Doubleday & McClure Company, 1899.

—-. "The Poet."

—-. "Two at a Fireside."

Mason, Caroline Atherton. "The Voyage."

McLeod, Malcolm James. *The Culture of Simplicity*. Fleming H. Revell Company, 1904.

Mencius. "Book VII. Tsin Sin. Part II." *The Chinese Classics: Vol. II containing The Works of Mencius*. By James Legge. 1861.

Meynell, Alice. "The Rhythm of Life." *The Rhythm of Life And Other Essays*. John Lane, 1897.

Mickle, William Julius. "Knowledge: An Ode." *The Poetical Works of William Julius Mickle*. Printed at the Stanhope Press, by Charles Whittingham, 1808.

Mill, John Stuart. *Nature, the Utility of Religion, and Theism*. Watts and Co., 1904.

Milnes, Richard Monckton. "Labour." *Poems of Many Years*. Edward Moxon, 1844.

—-. "Moments."

Milton, John. "Book VIII." *Paradise Lost*.

Molinos, Michael (or Miguel) de. "Of Internal and Mystical Silence." *The Spiritual Guide.* Translated from the Italian copy. Hodder and Stoughton, 1688.

Monsell, John S. B. *Spiritual Songs for the Sundays and Holydays Throughout the Year.* Parker, Son, and Bourn, 1861.

Montgomery, James. "Humility." *A Poet's Portfolio; or, Minor Poems: in Three Books.* Longman, Rees, Orme, Brown, Green, & Longman, 1835.

—-. "Time: A Rhapsody."

—-. "Prayer is the Soul's Sincere Desire". *A Church of England Hymn Book.* Compiled and edited by Godfrey Thring. W. Skeffington and Son, 1880.

Moore, Thomas. *The Loves of the Angels: A Poem.* R. Rhodes, 1823.

More, Hannah. "Sensibility: An Epistle to the Honourable Mrs. Boscawen." *Sacred Dramas.* P. Byrne, 1784.

Morgan, Angela. "Today."

—-. "Reality." *Utterance And Other Poems.* Dodd Mead, 1917.

Morley, John. *Aphorisms—an address delivered before the Edinburgh Philosophical Institution, November 11, 1887.* MacMillan and Co., 1887.

Morris, Lewis. *The Epic of Hades: In Three Books.* Roberts Brothers, 1879.

—-. *The Ode of Life.* C. Kegan Paul & Co., 1880.

—-. "The Ode of Change."

—-. "The Ode of Perfect Years."

Mountford, William. *Thorpe: A Quiet English Town, and Human Life Therein*. Ticknor, Reed and Fields, 1852.

Mudge, James. "Preface." *Poems with Power to Strengthen the Soul*. Abingdon-Cokesbury Press, 1909.

Mulford, Prentice. "Coarse Gold." *Michigan Argus*, 9 Jun. 1871.

Naidu, Sarojini. "A Challenge to Fate." *The Bird of Time. Songs of Life, Death & the Spring*. William Heinemann, 1912.

—-. "Guerdon."

—-. "Transience."

—-. "To a Buddha seated on a Lotus." *The Golden Threshold*. William Heinemann, 1905.

Novalis (Georg Philipp Friedrich Freiherr von Hardenberg). *From Forty Thousand Sublime and Beautiful Thoughts*. Compiled by Charles Noel Douglas. The Christian Herald, 1915.

Osgood, Frances Sargent. "Labour." *The Poets and Poetry of America: With an Historical Introduction*. By Rufus Wilmot Griswold. Carey and Hart, 1847.

—-. "Music." *The Female Poets of America*. By Rufus Wilmot Griswold. Henry C. Baird, 1853.

Ossoli, Margaret Fuller. "Thanksgiving." *Life Without and Life Within, Or, Reviews, Narratives, Essays, and Poems*. Brown, Taggard and Chase, 1859.

Parker, Theodore. "Books." *The Collected Works of Theodore Parker: Vol. XIV. Lessons from the World of Matter and the World of Man*. Trübner and Company, 1872.

—-. "Mind in the World of Matter."

Phelps, Egbert. "Life's Incongruities". *The Golden Treasury of Poetry and Prose*. Edited by Francis Fisher Browne. N.D. Thompson and Company, 1883.

Plato, Ann. "Reflections on the close of life." *Essays: Including Biographies and Miscellaneous Pieces in Prose and Poetry*. Ann Plato. 1841.

Plutarch. "On Contentedness of Mind." *Plutarch's Morals: Ethical Essays*. Translated with Notes and Index by Arthur Richard Shilleto. George Bell and Sons, 1898.

Poe, Edgar Allan. "The Poetic Principle." *The Complete Poetical Works of Edgar Allan Poe, with Memoir by J.H. Ingram*. International Book Company, 1866.

Poile, M. Frances. "Silence." *Mental Chemistry*. Charles Francis Haanel. 1922.

Pope, Alexander. *The Complete Poetical Works of Alexander Pope*. Houghton Mifflin Company, 1903.

—-. *An Essay on Criticism. Part 1*.

—-. *An Essay on Man. Moral Essays and Satires*. Cassell & Company, Limited, 1891.

Prince, John Critchley. *Hours with the Muses*. Simpkin, Marshall, and Co., 1841.

Prior, Matthew. *Solomon On The Vanity Of The World, A Poem. In Three Books*.

Procter, Adelaide Anne. "Friend Sorrow." *The Poems of Adelaide A. Procter*. With an introduction by Charles Dickens. John Wurtele Lovell, 1881.

—-. "Golden Words."

—-. "One by One."

Procter, Bryan Waller. "The Gauge of Life."

Reveley, Ida Louise. "My Riches." *The Christian Advocate*, 7 Oct. 1909, page 1585.

Rice, Grantland. "The Trainers" *Songs of the Stalwart*. D. Appleton and Company, 1917.

Riley, James Whitcomb. "Who Bides His Time."

Robertson, Frederick William. *Sermons Preached at Brighton*. Harper & Brothers, 1873.

Rousseau, Jean-Jacques. *Emile*. Book II.

Rumi (Jalāl ad-Dīn Muhammad Rūmī). "Remembered Music."

Saxe, John Godfrey. "The Library." *The Poems of John Godfrey Saxe*. James R. Osgood and Company, 1872.

—-. "The Poet's License."

Scott, Sir Walter. *The Waverley Novels*. *The Antiquary*.

Seneca, Lucius Annaeus. "Of a Happy Life." *Seneca's Morals of a Happy Life, Benefits, Anger, and Clemency*. Translated by Sir Roger L'Estrange. Belford, Clarke, & Co., 1882.

Shabistari, Mahmud. "Part IV. The Journey." *The Secret Rose Garden of Sa'd Ud Din Mahmud Shabistari*. Rendered from the Persian with an Introduction by Florence Lederer. J. Murray, 1920.

—-. "Part IX. Man: His Capabilities and His Destiny."

—-. "Part X. The One."

Shakespeare, William. *As You Like It.*

—-. *Henry VI. Part 3.*

—-. "Orpheus." *Henry VIII.*

—-. *Measure for Measure.*

—-. *The Merchant of Venice.*

Shelley, Percy Bysshe. "A Defence of Poetry." *A Defence of Poetry and Other Essays.*

Sigourney, Lydia Howard. "True Wisdom". *Pocahontas, and Other Poems.* Harper & Brothers, 1841.

Smiles, Samuel. *Character.* John Murray, 1871.

—-. *Duty: With Illustrations of Courage, Patience and Endurance.* John Murray, 1883.

—-. *Self-help; with illustrations of character and conduct.* John Murray, 1897.

Southwell, Robert. "Times go by Turns." *The Oxford Book of English Verse: 1250–1900.* Arthur Quiller-Couch, ed. 1919.

Stebbins, Horatio. *Borrowings, a Compilation of Helpful Thoughts from Great Authors.* William Doxey, 1891, p. 71.

Stoddard, Richard Henry. "Introduction." *The Golden Treasury of Poetry and Prose.* Edited by Francis Fisher Browne. N.D. Thompson and Company, 1883.

Street, Alfred Billings. "Nature." *The Poems of Alfred B. Street.* Clark & Austin, 1847.

Swain, Charles. "The Mind." *The Mind, and Other Poems.* Longman, Brown, Green, and Longmans, 1849.

—. "What is Noble?". *Selections from Charles Swain*. Arthur C. Fifield, 1906.

Swinburne, Algernon Charles. *Atalanta in Calydon: A Tragedy*. Ticknor and Fields, 1866.

Tagore, Rabindranath. *Gitanjali (Song Offerings)*. *A collection of prose translations made by the author from the original Bengali*. With an introduction by W. B. YEATS. Macmillan and Company, limited, 1914.

Tao Te Ching by Lao-Tzu, Complete online text, a translation for the public domain by J. H. McDonald. 1996.

Taylor, Ida Scott. *The Year Book of English Authors*. Written and Compiled by Ida Scott Taylor. H.M. Caldwell Co, 1894.

Taylor, Jane. "Prejudice." *Essays in Rhyme, on Morals and Manners*. Taylor and Hessey, 1820.

Taylor, Jeremy. *The Beauties of Jeremy Taylor, D.D. Selected from His Works*. Blackie & Son, 1834.

—. *Discourses on Various Subjects, Volume 1*. Wells and Lilly, 1816.

—. *The Rules and Exercises of Holy Living*. William Pickering, 1847.

—. *The Whole Works of the Right Rev. Jeremy Taylor*. Longman, Brown, Green, and Longmans, 1850.

—. *The Works of Jeremy Taylor D.D., Volume 1*. A. J. Valpy, 1831.

Tennyson, Alfred Lord. "Akbar's Dream." *The Death of Oenone, Akbar's Dream, and Other Poems*. Macmillan and Co. 1892.

Thaxter, Celia. "The Sunrise Never Failed Us Yet." *The Poems of Celia Thaxter*. Houghton, Mifflin and Company, 1896.

Thomson, James. *Coriolanus: A Tragedy*. John Exshaw, 1767.

Thoreau, Henry David. *Walden*.

Tilton, Theodore. "The Mystery of Nature." *The Sexton's Tale, and Other Poems*. Sheldon and Company, 1867.

Tolstoi, Count Leo. *My Religion*. Translated from the French by Huntington Smith. Thomas Y. Crowell & Co., 1885.

Trine, Ralph Waldo. *In Tune with the Infinite*. London George Bell & Sons, 1903.

Trotter, James M. "A Description of Music." *Music and Some Highly Musical People*. Lee and Shepard, 1881.

Trowbridge, John Townsend. "Twoscore and Ten." *A Home Idyl: And Other Poems*. Houghton, Mifflin and Company, The Riverside Press, 1881.

Tupper, Martin Farquhar. "My Own Place."

—-. "Of Compensation." *Proverbial Philosophy: A Book of Thoughts and Arguments*. John Wiley, 1850.

—-. "Of Gifts."

—-. "Of Humility."

—-. "Of Mystery."

—-. "Of Trifles."

Underhill, Evelyn. *The Essentials of Mysticism and Other Essays*. J.M. Dent & Sons Ltd, 1920.

—-. "The Essentials of Mysticism."

—-. "The Place of Will, Intellect, and Feeling in Prayer."

—-. "Introduction." *Songs of Kabir*. Translated by Rabindranath Tagore. The Macmillan Company, 1915.

Van Dyke, Henry. "God of the Open Air." *Music and Other Poems*. C. Scribner's Sons, 1908.

Wagner, Charles. *The Better Way*. Translated from the French by Mary Louise Hendee. McClure, Phillips, and Co., 1904.

—-. *The Simple Life*. Translated from the French by Mary Louise Hendee. McClure, Phillips & Company, 1901.

Walkley, A. B. "Introduction". *The Treasure of the Humble*. By Maurice Maeterlinck. Translated by Alfred Sutro. With Introduction by A. B. Walkley. George Allen, Ruskin House, 1905.

Waterman, Nixon. "This Busy World." *The Girl Wanted*. Forbes and Company, 1919.

Wheatley, Phillis. "Thoughts on the Works of Providence." *Poems on Various Subjects, Religious and Moral*. W.H. Lawrence & Company, 1887.

Whitfield, James Monroe. "Ode To Music."

Whitman, Albery Allson. "Canto 1. Invocation." *The Rape of Florida*. Nixon-Jones Printing Company, 1884.

—-. "Dedicatory Address."

Whitman, Walt. "Song of Joys." *Leaves of Grass*. Doubleday, Page and Company, 1917.

Whittier, John Greenleaf. "Giving and Taking." *The Poetical Works of John Greenleaf Whittier*.

—-. "The Worship of Nature." *The Complete Poetical Works*

of Whittier. Edited by Horace Elisha Scudder. Houghton, Mifflin and Company, 1894.

Wilcox, Ella Wheeler. "The Last Dance". *Poems of Optimism*. Gay and Hancock, Ltd., 1919.

—-. "Life's Harmonies." *Poems of Power*. W. B. Conkey Company, 1902.

—-. "Morning Prayer."

—-. "Will."

Wordsworth, William. "Book Fourth. Despondency Corrected." *The Excursion*.

—-. "Lines Written a Few Miles Above Tintern Abbey." *Lyrical Ballads, with a Few Other Poems*. J. & A. Arch, 1798.

—-. *Ode on Intimations of Immortality: From Recollections of Early Childhood*.

—-. *Poems of Wordsworth*.

   —-. "Mutability."

   —-. "Ode to Duty."

   —-. "The Tables Turned."

—-. *The Prelude, or Growth of a Poet's Mind*. D.C. Heath and Co., 1888.

Young, Edward. *Love of Fame, The Universal Passion. In Seven Characteristical Satires*. J. and R. Tonson, 1752.

www.ingramcontent.com/pod-product-compliance
Lightning Source LLC
LaVergne TN
LVHW021654060526
838200LV00050B/2348